KAREN BROWN'S

English, Welsh & Scottish Country Hotels & Itineraries

OTHER KAREN BROWN TITLES

Austrian Country Inns & Castles

California Country Inns & Itineraries

English Country Bed & Breakfasts

English, Welsh & Scottish Country Hotels & Itineraries

French Country Bed & Breakfasts

French Country Inns & Itineraries

German Country Inns & Itineraries

Irish Country Inns

Italian Country Bed & Breakfasts

Italian Country Inns & Itineraries

Portuguese Country Inns & Pousadas

Scandinavian Country Inns & Manors

Spanish Country Inns & Paradors

Swiss Country Inns & Chalets

KAREN BROWN'S

English, Welsh & Scottish Country Hotels & Itineraries

Written by

JUNE BROWN and KAREN BROWN

Sketches by Barbara Tapp

Cover Art by Jann Pollard

Karen Brown's Country Inn Series

Editors: Karen Brown, Clare Brown, June Brown, Iris Sandilands
Technical support: William H. Brown III; Aide-de-camp: William H. Brown
Illustrations: Barbara Tapp; Cover Painting: Jann Pollard; Maps: Cassell Design

Written in cooperation with Town and Country - Hillsdale Travel, San Mateo, CA

Copyright © 1980, 1985, 1986, 1987, 1988, 1992 Karen Brown's Guides

Distributed by The Globe Pequot Press, 138 West Main Street, Chester, CT 06412

Library of Congress Cataloging-in-Publication Data

Brown, Karen.
    Karen Brown's English, Welsh & Scottish country hotels &
itineraries / written by June Brown and Karen Brown ; sketches by
Barbara Tapp ; cover art by Jann Pollard.
      p.   cm. -- (Karen Brown's country inn series)
    Rev. ed. of: English, Welsh & Scottish country inns / June & Karen
Brown. Updated and rev. 5th ed. c1988.
    Includes index.
    ISBN 0-930328-00-0 : $14.95
    1. Hotels, taverns, etc. --England--Guide-books. 2. Hotels,
taverns, etc.--Wales--Guide-books. 3. Hotels, taverns, etc.-
-Scotland--Guide-books. 4. England--Description and travel--1971- -
-Guide-books. 5. Wales--Description and travel--1981- -- Guide
-books. 6. Scotland--Description and travel--1981- --Guide-books.
I. Brown, June, 1949- II. Brown, June, 1949- English, Welsh &
Scottish country inns. III. Title. IV. Title: English, Welsh &
Scottish country hotels & itineraries. V. Title: Karen Brown's
English, Welsh, and Scottish country hotels and itineraries. VI.Title:
English, Welsh, and Scottish country hotels and itineraries. VII. Series
TX907.5.G7B76 1992
647.944101--dc20   91-40773
                                                                  CIP

To my children

Simon and Clare

in the hope that they will

discover Britain for themselves

Contents

Hotels

Introduction

This guide falls into three sections: practical information useful in planning your trip; driving itineraries that take you deep into the countryside through idyllic villages full of thatched-roofed cottages and flower-filled gardens, exploring ancient castles and traversing vast purple moorlands; and lastly, but most importantly, our personal recommendations for outstanding hotels in England, Scotland, and Wales. Every hotel included in this guide is one that we have seen and enjoyed--our personal recommendation written with the sincere belief that where you lay your head each night makes the difference between a good and a great vacation. If you prefer to travel the bed and breakfast way, you may prefer to select places to stay from our companion guide, *English Country Bed & Breakfasts*. We encourage you to buy new editions of our guides and throw away old ones--you will be glad you did because we add new listings, update prices, phone and fax numbers, and delete places that have not maintained standards.

Car Rental: If you are coming from overseas it is frequently less expensive to arrange and prepay a car rental before arriving in Britain. Car companies in collaboration with airlines often offer a variety of rental packages. Plan on visiting London either at the beginning or end of your trip. This way you can arrive in London, pick you car up at the airport, tour the countryside, drop the car back at the airport, and take a taxi, the bus or tube from Heathrow, or the train from Gatwick Airport into London. If you visit London at the start of your holiday collect your car from the airport at the conclusion of your stay in London. The trick is to avoid driving in London.

Driving: Just about the time overseas visitors board their return flight home they will have adjusted to driving on the "right" side which is the left side in England. You must contend with such things as roundabouts (circular intersections); flyovers (overpasses); ring roads (peripheral roads whose purpose is to bypass city traffic); lorries (trucks); lay-bys (turn-outs); boots (trunks); and bonnets (hoods). Pedestrians are permitted to cross the road anywhere and always have the right of way. Seat belts must be worn at all times.

Motorways: The letter "M" precedes these convenient ways to cover long distances. With three lanes of traffic either side of a central divider you should stay in the left-hand lane except for passing. Motorway exits are numbered and correspond to numbering on major road maps. Service areas supply petrol, cafeterias, and "bathrooms" (the word "bathroom" is used in the American sense--in Britain "bathroom" means a room with a shower or bathtub, not a toilet--"loo" is the most commonly used term for an American bathroom).

"A" Roads: The letter "A" precedes the road number. All major roads fall into this category. They vary from three lanes either side of a dividing barrier to single carriageways with an unbroken white line in the middle indicating that passing is not permitted. These roads have the rather alarming habit of changing from dual to single carriageways at a moment's notice.

2   *Introduction*

"B" Roads and Country Roads: The letter "B" preceding the road number or the lack of any lettering or numbering indicates that it belongs to the maze of country roads that crisscross Britain.   These are the roads for people who have the luxury of time to enjoy the scenery en route.   Arm yourself with a good map (although getting lost is part of the adventure).   Driving these narrow roads is terrifying at first but exhilarating after a while.   Meandering down these roads, you can expect to spend time crawling behind a tractor or cows being herded to the farmyard. Some lanes are so narrow that there is room for only one car.

Electricity: The voltage is 240.   Most bathrooms have razor points (American style) for 110 volts.   If you are coming from overseas it is recommended that you take only dual voltage appliances and a kit of electrical plugs.   Often your host can loan you a hairdryer and an iron.

Hotel Descriptions: The third section of this guide contains our recommendations for outstanding places to stay in England, Scotland, and Wales.   Each listing is very different and occasionally the owners have their eccentricities, which all adds to the allure of these small hotels.   We have tried to be candid and honest in our appraisals and tried to convey each hotel's special flavor so that you know what to expect and will not be disappointed.   No hotel pays to be included in our guide, they are all places that we have visited, inspected and stayed--places that we enjoy. Our recommendations cover a wide range: please do not expect the same standard of luxury at, for example, the lovely Wykeman Arms in Winchester as at the luxurious Chewton Glen--there is no comparison--yet each is outstanding in what it offers.   We have tried to mention major sightseeing attractions near each countryside listing to encourage you to spend several nights in each location.   Few countries have as much to offer as Great Britain--within a few miles of most listings there are places of interest to visit and explore--lofty cathedrals, quaint churches, museums, and grand country houses.

Hotels and Children: Places that welcome children state *Children welcome*. The majority of listings in this guide do not "welcome" children but find they become tolerable at different ages over 5 or, more often than not, over 12. In some cases places simply do not accept children and the listing states *No children*. However, these indications of children's acceptability are not cast in stone, so if you have your heart set on staying at a listing that states *Children over 12* and you have an 8-year-old, call them, explain your situation, and they may well accept you. Ideally we would like to see all listings welcoming children and all parents remembering that they are staying in a hotel and doing their bit by making sure that children do not run wild.

Hotels' Christmas Programs: Several listings offer Christmas getaways--if the information section indicates that the listing is open during the Christmas season, there is a very good chance that it offers a festive Christmas package.

Hotels & Credit Cards: Whether hotels accepts payment by credit card is indicated using the terms *AX*-American Express, *MC*-Master Card, *VS*-Visa, or simply *all major*.

Hotel Directions: We give concise driving directions to guide you to the listing which is often in a more out-of-the-way place than the town or village in the address. We would be very grateful if you would let us know of cases where our directions have proved inadequate.

Hotel Rates: Rates are those quoted to us for the 1992 summer season. We have tried to standardize rates by quoting the 1992 rate for a standard single and a standard double room. Not all places conform so where dinner is included, or the listing only quotes per person rates we have stated this in the listing. Prices are always quoted to include breakfast, Value Added Tax (VAT), and service (if these are applicable). Please use the figures printed as a guideline and be certain to ask what the rate is at the time of booking. Many listings offer special terms, below their normal prices, for "short breaks" of two or more nights. In many listings suites are available at higher prices.

Hotel Reservations: Reservations can be confining and usually must be guaranteed by a deposit; however, if you have your heart set on a particular place, to avoid disappointment make a reservation. If you prefer to travel as whim and the weather dictate, rooms can often be had in the countryside with just a few days' notice. July and August are the busiest times and if you are travelling to a popular spot such as Bath or York, it is advisable to make reservations. It is always a good idea to have reservations in London.

It is completely unacceptable practice to make reservations for a particular night at several establishments, choosing at the last minute which one to stay at.

Although proprietors do not always strictly adhere to it, it is important to understand that once reservations are confirmed--whether by phone or in writing--you are under contract. This means that the proprietor is legally obligated to provide the accommodation he has promised and that you are bound to pay for that accommodation. If you cannot take up your accommodation, you are liable for a portion of the accommodation charges plus your deposit. If you have to cancel your reservation, do so as soon as possible so that the proprietor can attempt to re-let your room--in which case you are liable only for the re-let fee or the deposit. There are several options for making hotel reservations:

Letter: If you write for reservations, state clearly exactly what you want, how many people are in your party, how many rooms you require, the category of room you prefer (standard, superior, deluxe), and your date of arrival and departure and enquire about deposit requirements. The hotel usually sends you a map with your confirmation. When you receive a reply send your deposit.

Fax: If you have access to a fax machine, this is a very quick way to reach a hotel. If the hotel has a fax we have included the number in the listing.

Telephone: If you are visiting from overseas, our preference for making a reservation is by telephone; the cost is minimal and you have your answer immediately, so if space is not available, you can then decide on an alternate. (If calling from the United States, allow for the time difference [England is five hours ahead of New York] so that you can call during their business day. Dial 011 [the international code], 44 [Britain's code], then the city code [dropping the 0] and the telephone number.) Be specific as to what your needs are, such as a ground-floor room, ensuite bathroom or twin beds. Check the prices which may well have changed from those given in the book (summer 1992). Ask what deposit to send or give your credit card number. Tell them approximately what time you intend to arrive and request dinner if you want it. Ask for a confirmation letter with brochure and map to be sent to you.

U.S. Representative: Many of the hotels have United States representatives, often more than one. We have listed the U.S. representatives along with the hotels they book beginning on page 235. This is an extremely convenient way to secure a reservation. However, sometimes representatives make a charge for their services, or only reserve the more expensive rooms, or quote a higher price to protect themselves against currency fluctuations.

Introduction

Information: The British Tourist Authority is an invaluable source of information. Offices are located in the United States and Canada at:

ATLANTA: The British Tourist Authority, #470, 2580 Cumberland Parkway, Atlanta, GA 30339, tel (404) 432-9635

CHICAGO: The British Tourist Authority, #1510, 625 North Michigan Ave., Chicago, IL 60611, tel (312) 787-0490

LOS ANGELES: The British Tourist Authority, World Trade Center, 350 South Figueroa St., Suite 450, Los Angeles, CA 90071, tel (213) 628-3525

NEW YORK: The British Tourist Authority, 40 West 57th Street, 3rd floor, New York, NY 10019, tel (212) 581-4700

TORONTO: The British Tourist Authority, 94 Cumberland Street, Suite 600, Toronto, Ontario M5R 3N3, tel (416) 925-6326.

If you need additional information while you are in Britain there are more than 700 official Tourist Information Centres identified by a blue and white letter "i" and "Tourist Information." These centers are invaluable sources for books, maps, and pamphlets on their local area. Many information centers will make reservations for local accommodation and larger ones will "book a bed ahead" in a different locality.

In London the British Travel Centre at 4-12 Lower Regent Street, London SW1 (near Piccadilly Circus tube station) provides information on what to see and do, and how to do it, all year round in Britain. You can book a room, buy air or train tickets, hire a car or pay for a coach tour or theatre tickets in one location. The Centre also has changing exhibitions and a "video wall" where several screens display films of attractions to be found round the country. The Centre is open 9 am to 6:30 pm Monday to Saturday, 10 am to 4:00 pm on Sunday.

Overview Map of Driving Itineraries

Scotland

Edinburgh

The Lake District

North Yorkshire

York

Derbyshire Dales & Villages

Chester

Chesterfield

Ashbourne

Cambridge & East Anglia

Wales

Coventry

Cambridge

Oxford

Bath

LONDON

Southwest England

Winchester

Exeter

Portsmouth

Southeast England

Introduction

Itineraries: Nine driving itineraries map a route through the various regions of England, Wales, and Scotland.   Rather than suggest a specific pace, each itinerary map, which precedes the text, shows all of the towns in which we have a recommended hotel.   Often all, or a large portion, of an itinerary can be enjoyed using one hotel as a base and staying for several days.

Most sightseeing venues operate a *summer* and a *winter* opening regime, the changeover occurring around late March/early April and late October/early November.   If you happen to be visiting at the changeover times, be sure to check whether your chosen venue is open before making plans.   We try to give an indication of opening times.   However, there is every possibility that these dates and times will have changed by the time you plan your trip so before you embark on an excursion, check the dates and hours of opening.

Maps: Each driving itinerary is preceded by a map showing the route and each hotel listing is referenced to a map at the back of the book.   These are an artist's renderings and are not intended to replace commercial maps.   Our suggestion is to purchase a large-scale road atlas of England where an inch equals 10 miles. English hotel maps in this book can be cross referenced with those in our companion guide *English Country Bed & Breakfasts*.

The National Trust: The National Trust works for the preservation of places of historic interest or national beauty in England, Wales, Northern Ireland, and Scotland.   Its care extends to stately homes, barns, historic houses, castles, gardens, Roman antiquities, moors, fells, woods, and even whole villages.   During the course of a driving itinerary, whenever a property is under the care of the National Trust we state (NT).   You can check times and location with the current edition of *The National Trust Handbook* available from many National Trust shops and overseas from the British Tourist Authority.   If you are travelling to Scotland, you will need a copy of *The National Trust for Scotland Guide*.   A great many

National Trust properties have excellent shops and tearooms. If you are planning on visiting several properties consider joining the National Trust as a member, thus obtaining free entry into all properties.

Shopping: Overseas visitors can reclaim the VAT (Value Added Tax) that they pay on the goods they purchase. Not all stores participate in the refund scheme and there is often a minimum purchase price. Stores that do participate will ask to see your passport before completing the VAT form. This form must be presented with the goods to the Customs officer at the point of departure from Britain within three months of purchase. The customs officer will certify the form which you return to the store where you bought the goods. The store will then send you a check in sterling for the refund.

Weather: Britain has a tendency to be moist at all times of the year. The cold in winter is rarely severe; however, the farther north you go the greater the possibility of being snowed in. Spring can be wet but it is a lovely time to travel: the summer crowds have not descended, daffodils and bluebells fill the woodlands, and the hedgerows are filled with wildflowers. Summer offers the best chance of sunshine but also the largest crowds. Schools are usually closed the last two weeks of July and all of August--this is the time when most families take their summer holidays. Travel is especially hectic on the weekends in summer--try to avoid major routes and airports at these times. Autumn is also an ideal touring time: the weather tends to be drier than in spring and the woodlands are decked in their golden fall finery.

The Heart of England

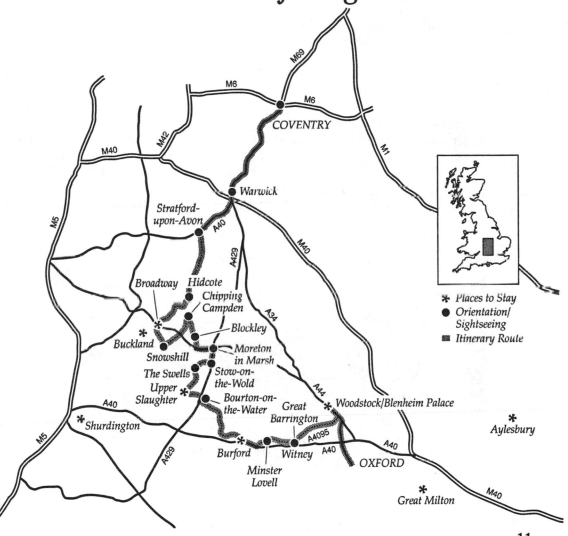

COVENTRY

Warwick

Stratford-
upon-Avon

Broadway Hidcote

Chipping
Campden

Blockley

Buckland

Snowshill

Moreton
in Marsh

The Swells

Stow-on-
the-Wold

Upper
Slaughter

Bourton-on-
the-Water

Great
Barrington

Woodstock/Blenheim Palace

Shurdington

Aylesbury

Burford Witney

OXFORD

Minster
Lovell

Great Milton

* Places to Stay
● Orientation/
   Sightseeing
▨ Itinerary Route

The Heart of England

From the gracious university town of Oxford through the quintessentially English Cotswold villages to Shakespearean Stratford and the grand fortress of Warwick Castle, this itinerary covers famous attractions and idyllic countryside nooks and crannies. The Cotswolds is a region of one sleepy village after another clad in the local soft-gray limestone or creamy-golden ironstone, where mellow stone walls, manor houses, and churches cluster along river banks, perch on steep-sided hills, or scatter independently in a pocket of a pretty valley. In Shakespeare's day this was sheep country and the center of England's wool industry. By the mid-1800s the area had fallen into decline, its wool trade usurped by Australia and New Zealand. And thus the area slept, by-passed by the factories and cities of the Industrial Revolution. Now tourists flock to the Cotswolds and yet the region remains remarkably unspoilt: in fact, it appears to thrive on the attention and popularity.

Lower Slaughter

OXFORD is a beautiful university town, graced by spacious lawns, pretty parks, lacy spires, honey-colored Cotswold stones, romantic pathways, and two picturesque rivers--the Cherwell and the Thames. Follow signs for the city center, park in any of the well-signposted, multistory car parks and foray on foot to explore. You may want to make your first stop the Oxford Information Centre, on St Aldates, across from the town hall, to obtain a map and information (*tel 0865-726873*). Much of the sightseeing in this the oldest university town centers on its colleges whose open times depend on whether the students are "up" (there) or "down" (not there). Particularly worth visiting are CHRIST CHURCH COLLEGE with its superb quad and tower designed by Wren to hold the bell Great Tom; MAGDALEN COLLEGE, the most beautiful college, with its huge gardens making you feel as if you are in the countryside; and MERTON COLLEGE whose chapel contains 13th- to 14th-century glass. Apart from the colleges, visit ST MARY'S CHURCH where you can climb the spire for a marvelous view of the city; the ASHMOLEAN MUSEUM with its remarkable collection of paintings, tapestries, and sculptures; the riverside BOTANICAL GARDENS opposite Magdalen College; BLACKWELL'S, the most famous of Oxford's many book stores; and THE BEAR, on Alfred Street, a marvelous old pub dating from 1242. Punts can be rented on the River Cherwell from beside Magdalen Bridge.

Leaving Oxford, take the A34 (Stratford-Upon-Avon) to WOODSTOCK, one of England's prettiest country towns. On the outskirts of Woodstock are the famous gates of BLENHEIM PALACE, Sir John Vanbrugh's masterpiece, which was built for John Churchill, the 1st Duke of Marlborough. The construction of the house was a gift from Queen Anne to the Duke after his victory over the French and Bavarians at Blenheim in 1704. However, before its completion, Queen Anne's gratitude had waned and the Marlborough family had to pay to have the house finished. The gardens and park-like grounds were landscaped by Capability Brown. Sir Winston Churchill, the grandson of the 7th Duke, was born here on November 30, 1874, and associations with him have accented the historical interest of the Palace. (Winston Churchill, his wife, father, Lord Randolph Churchill, and mother, Jenny Jerome, the beautiful daughter of an American newspaper owner, are buried in St Martin's churchyard in Bladon, 2 miles away.) You drive through the grounds to the house, park on the lawn, and either tour the sumptuous rooms with a group or wander independently. A narrow-gauge railway takes you through the park to the butterfly farm and plant center. (*Open mid-March-October, tel 0993-811325.*) In contrast to the immense palace and spacious grounds are the compact streets of the little town of Woodstock with its coaching inns, delightful hotel (The Feathers), and interesting shops.

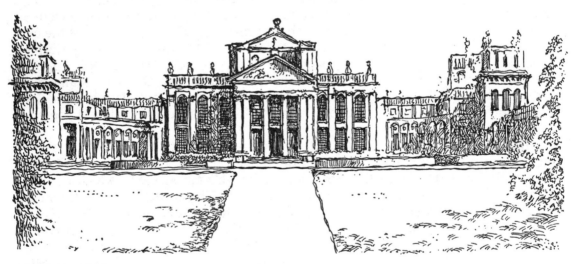

Blenheim Palace

Retrace your steps for a short distance on the A34 in the direction of Oxford and take the A4095 for 7 miles to the mellow, stone town of WITNEY where blankets

The Heart of England

have been made for over a thousand years and which still preserves its Cotswold market-town atmosphere. The 18th-century Blanket Hall was used for weighing blankets and has an unusual one-handed clock.

MINSTER LOVELL is a few miles to the west along the B4047: to reach the old part of the village follow the brown signs for "Minster Lovell Hall." Park at the end of the lane and walk through the churchyard to see the ruined home of the Lovell family, in a field by the river's edge. Some people arrive in Minster Lovell because they have heard it is one of the loveliest villages on the River Windrush, while others are attracted by the reputation of a charming, 500-year-old inn, The Old Swan, and its excellent restaurant. Leave the village by the road to the side of The Swan, following signs through ASTALL LEIGH and ASTALL to the A40 which you take in the direction of Cheltenham for a short distance to Burford.

Follow signs for "tourist information" which bring you down the hill into the lovely "olde-worlde" Cotswold town of BURFORD. The broad High Street sweeps down the hillside, bordered by numerous antique and gift shops, to the bridge spanning the River Windrush. Branching off are delightful, narrow residential streets with flower-filled cottage gardens. In the days when coach and horses were the main form of transport, Burford was a way station. The coaches are long gone but the lovely inns remain: two with the most atmosphere are The Bay Tree and the adjacent Lamb Inn.

Explore Burford and leave town following the road over the River Windrush. Go left at the mini roundabout, directing yourself down country lanes to TAYNTON with its adorable thatched and golden stone cottages and on up the valley to GREAT BARRINGTON and LITTLE BARRINGTON, a village of quaint cottages grouped round a grassy hollow. Turn right along the A40 towards Cheltenham and first right to WINDRUSH where you pick up signs for the drive down country lanes through SHERBOURNE to Bourton-on-the-Water. (When you come to the A429 turn right and then right into Bourton-on-the-Water)

BOURTON-ON-THE-WATER is a lovely village with a number of riverside greens and low bridges spanning the River Windrush. Go early in the morning, just before sunset, or in the winter to avoid the crowds that overrun this peaceful (albeit somewhat over-commercialized) spot.

Leave Bourton-on-the-Water by going down the main street and turning right for a very short distance on the A429 (in the direction of Cheltenham) to a left-hand turn which directs you down country lanes to the more peaceful side of the Cotswolds as typified by the outstandingly lovely villages of LOWER and UPPER SLAUGHTER with their honey-colored stone cottages beside peaceful streams--just the names on the signpost are enough to lure you down their lanes. From Upper Slaughter follow signs for Stow-on-the-Wold down country lanes through the "the Swells," LOWER and UPPER SWELL, other picturesque examples of villages with whimsical names.

STOW-ON-THE-WOLD, its market square lined by mellow, old gray-stoned buildings, was one of the most prosperous wool towns in England. Most of the 17th-century buildings around the square now house interesting shops. Two of Stow's main thoroughfares--Sheep Street and Shepherds Way--are reminders that selling sheep was once the town's main livelihood. Cromwell converted the 12th-century church into a prison and used it to hold 1000 Royalists captive after a Civil War battle in 1646.

Nearby MORETON IN MARSH's broad main street which was once part of the Roman road known as the Fosse Way is lined with interesting shops. At the crossroads take the A44 towards Evesham to BOURTON-ON-THE-HILL, an appropriately named village whose houses climb a steep hillside. At the top of the hill turn right for BLOCKLEY and follow signs for the village center until you pick up signs for BROAD CAMPDEN and CHIPPING CAMPDEN, adorable 14th-century wool villages peppered with heavily thatched cottages. Detour to Chipping Campden's High Street lined with gabled cottages and shops topped by steep tile roofs. Woolstaplers Hall is now a museum of photographic and medical

The Heart of England

equipment and home of the tourist information center.

Cross the A44 and a country lane brings you to SNOWSHILL and SNOWSHILL MANOR (NT), a Tudor manor packed with collections of musical instruments, clocks, toys, and bicycles. *(Open May-September, closed Mondays and Tuesdays, tel 0386-852410.)*

Just down the lane flowers dress the lovely, weathered, stone-built houses of BROADWAY, a town which is often described as the perfection of Cotswold beauty. THE LYGON ARMS is as famous as the town, a magnificent 14th- to 16th-century hotel whose public rooms are exquisitely furnished with antiques. In summer the town is thronged with tourists so it is best to visit early or late in the day.

Turn right up the main street and first left on the B4632 (signposted Stratford), through peaceful WILLERSEY where ducks sail serenely on the village mere and WESTON-SUB-EDGE, to the outskirts of MICKLETON where you turn right for HIDCOTE MANOR GARDENS (NT), one of the most delightful gardens in England. Created early this century by Major Lawrence Johnston, it is a series of individual gardens each bounded by sculpted hedges and linked paths and terraces. Each "mini garden" focuses on a specific theme or flower. There are stunning displays of old roses and in summer the perennials are a blaze of color. *(Open March-October, closed Tuesdays and Fridays, tel 0386-438333.)* Next door, another outstanding garden, KIFTSGATE COURT, has exquisite displays of roses. *(Open April-September, Wednesday, Thursday, and Sunday.)*

Leaving Hidcote, return to Mickleton and turn right onto the B4632 into STRATFORD-UPON-AVON, the birthplace of the greatest poet of the English language, William Shakespeare. Stratford-upon-Avon is always impossibly crowded with visitors--if crowds are not to your liking, give it a miss. William Shakespeare was born in 1564 in a half-timbered house on Henley Street, educated at the King's New Grammar School and, in 1597, six years before his death, he retired to NEW PLACE, one of the finest and largest houses in Stratford. Simply engraved stones in front of the altar of the HOLY TRINITY CHURCH mark the burial spot of Shakespeare and some other members of his family. It is a fairly large town, with beautifully renovated timbered buildings and lovely shops to investigate. The town's glory, however, is brought expertly to the stage at the ROYAL SHAKESPEARE THEATRE and at its associate theatre, THE OTHER PLACE. (*Open April-December.*)

Warwick Castle

The Heart of England

Anne Hathaway married William Shakespeare in 1582, but until then she lived in a darling thatched cottage at SHOTTERY, a small town only a heartbeat away from Stratford-upon-Avon. You will see paintings and photographs of this picture-book cottage all over the world. (*Open all year.*)

When you leave Shottery head back towards the center of Stratford and take the A46 to WARWICK. WARWICK CASTLE is a magnificent, 14th-century fortress of formidable towers and turrets. The fortress dominates a choice spot on the river bank and its striking structure is beautifully preserved. Climb the towers, explore the armory and torture chamber below, then visit the Manor House. As you walk through the house you see what it was like to attend a house party given by the Earl and Countess of Warwick in 1898. The house has retained its period furniture and Madame Tussaud's has populated the rooms with wax figures from the past. Here a servant pours bathwater into a bath for a guest while downstairs guests listen to a recital being given by Dame Clara Butt. The gardens are decorated by arrogant, strutting peacocks. (*Open all year, tel 0926-492797.*)

Wander into Warwick with its mixture of Georgian and old, timber-frame houses. At the town's west gate stands the LEYCESTER HOSPITAL, for 400 years an almshouse for crippled soldiers. (*Closed Sundays, tel 0926-492797.*) In Beauchamp Chapel lies the tomb of Elizabeth I's favorite, the Earl of Leicester.

The large industrial city of COVENTRY lies just to the north--it is worth a visit to see COVENTRY CATHEDRAL, one of Europe's finest examples of modern architecture. On a night in 1940 Hitler's bombers destroyed 40 acres of the city center, including the cathedral. A new city center and a new cathedral were built after the war. The blackened ruins of the old cathedral form the approach to the new, with a cross made of two charred roof timbers on the old altar, inscribed "Father Forgive." In the new cathedral magnificent stained glass windows by modern artists all lead the eye to a massive stone altar with its abstract cross and crucifix. Behind it is a 75ft-tapestry of the "Redeeming Savior of the World." From Coventry fast motorways will connect you to all parts of Britain.

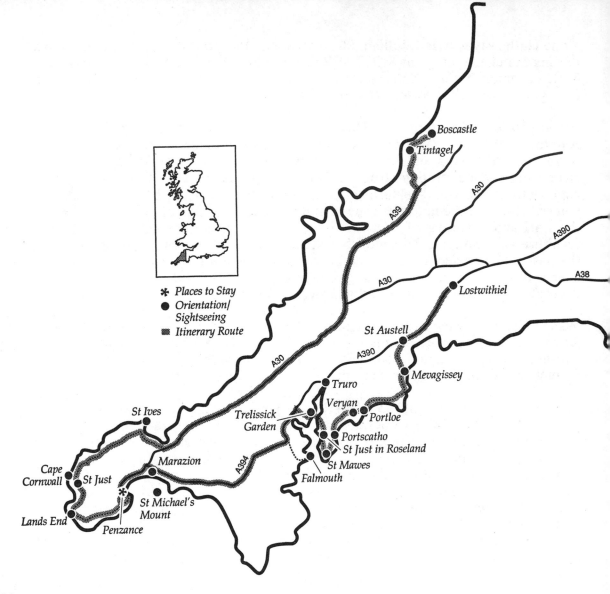

Places to Stay
● **Orientation/
  Sightseeing**
▨ **Itinerary Route**

Boscastle

Tintagel

A30

A39

A390

A38

A30

Lostwithiel

St Austell

A30

A390

Mevagissey

Truro

Veryan

Trelissick
Garden

Portloe

Portscatho

St Just in Roseland

St Ives

Marazion

St Mawes

A394

Falmouth

Cape
Cornwall

St Just

Lands End

Penzance

St Michael's
Mount

Southwest England

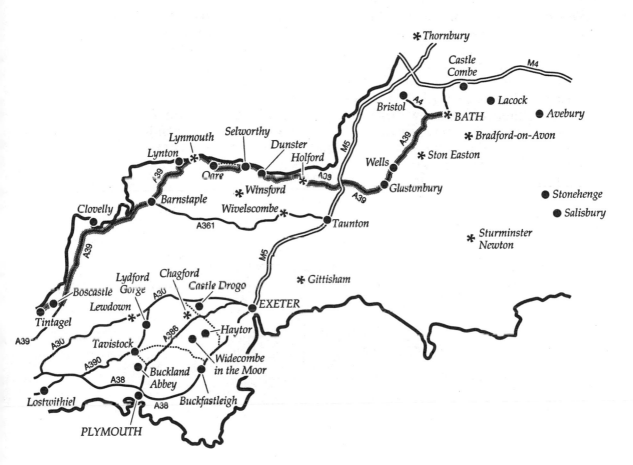

* Thornbury

Castle
Combe

M4

Bristol

A4

Lacock

* BATH

* Avebury

* Bradford-on-Avon

M5

Lynmouth   Selworthy

Lynton   Dunster
              Holford

Wells

* Ston Easton

A39

Oare

* Winsford

Glastonbury

Clovelly   Barnstaple

Wivelscombe *

A39

A361

Taunton

* Stonehenge

* Salisbury

* Sturminster
  Newton

A39

M5

* Gittisham

Lydford   Chagford
Gorge
Lewdown   Castle Drogo

Boscastle

A30

EXETER

Tintagel

A39   A30

Tavistock

A386

Haytor

A390   Widecombe
                    in the Moor

Lostwithiel   A38   Buckland
              Abbey

A38   Buckfastleigh

PLYMOUTH

Southwest England

Scenery changes noticeably as this itinerary traverses England southwest from Bath through Somerset and along its unspoilt coast, outlining Cornwall, into the heart of Devon. Wild Exmoor ponies gallop across the expanses of Exmoor. Along the coastline, the scenery changes dramatically from wooded inlets dropping to the sea to wild rollers crashing on granite cliffs, giving credence to old tales of wreckers luring ships onto rocky shorelines. Picturesque villages surround sheltered harbors, their quays strewn with nets and lobster pots. Southern ports present a gentler scene: bobbing yachts dot wooded estuaries and gentle waves lap the shoreline. Hedgerow-lined lanes meander inland across Dartmoor's heather-clad moorlands to picturesque towns nestling at her edge. Relax and enjoy your explorations of this westernmost spur of land jutting out into the Atlantic Ocean.

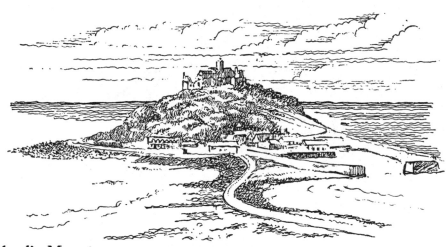

St Michael's Mount

The elegant city of BATH with its graceful, honey-colored buildings, interesting museums, and delightful shopping area is best explored on foot over a period of several days.   Bath, founded by the Romans in the 1st century around the gushing mineral hot springs, reached its peak of popularity in the early 1700s with the arrival of Beau Nash who opened the first Pump Room where people could take the water and socialize.   Yorkshire architects John Wood, father and son, used the local honey-colored stone to build the elegant streets and crescents in neoclassical Palladian style.

Maps are available from the Tourist Information Centre near the abbey (corner of Cheap and Stall Streets).   Entry into the ROMAN BATHS is via the PUMP ROOM which was the place to gather in the 18th and 19th centuries.   The Great Bath, a large warm swimming pool, built around a natural hot spring, now open to the sky, was once covered.   Mosaics, monuments, and many interesting artifacts from the town can be seen in the adjacent museum. (*Open all year, tel 0225-461111 ext 2782.*)

Nearby, tucked into a narrow passageway between Abbey Green and North Parade, is SALLY LUNN'S HOUSE a museum and a teashop.   The museum, in the cellar, has the kitchen preserved much as it was in the 1680s when Sally's buns and other baked goods were the favorites of Bath society.   Upstairs you can try a freshly baked Sally Lunn bun.

Eighteenth-century society came to be seen at balls and gatherings at the ASSEMBLY ROOMS and authors such as Austen, Smolett, and Fielding captured the social importance of these events.   The MUSEUM OF COSTUME, in the Assembly Rooms basement, should not be missed. (*Open all year, tel 0225-46111 ext 2782.*)

From the Museum of Costume it is an easy walk via The Circus, a tight circle lined with splendid houses designed by John Wood I, and Brock Street to the ROYAL CRESCENT, a great arc of 30 terrace houses that epitomize the Georgian elegance of Bath and are the prime example of John Wood II's architecture. ONE ROYAL CRESCENT has been authentically restored to the 18th-century style and contains an interesting kitchen museum and a gift shop. (*Open all year, tel 0225-428126.*)

Bath has some wonderful restaurants and delightful shops and boutiques: whether you are in the market for antiques or high fashion you will find shopping here a real joy.

While our itinerary takes us south and west from Bath, there are a great many interesting places to the east, listed below, that can easily be visited as daytrips from this lovely city.

The village of AVEBURY (NT), made up of a church, several houses, shops, and an old pub, lies within a vast circle of standing stones surrounded by earthworks. The site covers 28 acres. Unlike Stonehenge, where the stones are larger, the site smaller, and the crowds sometimes overwhelming, Avebury is a peaceful spot where, armed with a map, you can wander amongst the stones and wonder why about 4,000 years ago Bronze Age man spent what has been estimated at 1 1/2 million man hours to construct such a temple. (Just off the A4 between Calne & Marlborough.) (*Open all year, tel 06723-555.*)

CASTLE COMBE is the most photogenic collection of warm, honey, stone cottages snuggled along a stream's edge. (Just south of the M4 motorway between exits 18 and 17.)

CLAVERTON MANOR is the American museum in the United Kingdom. Furniture, household equipment, and period rooms show home life in the United States from the 17th to 19th centuries. (3 miles east of Bath.) (*Open April-October, tel 0225-460503.*)

LACOCK (NT) is an exquisite village where no building dates from later than the 18th century and many date from much earlier. Be sure to visit the Fox Talbot museum of early photographs and Lacock Abbey. The abbey was converted to a manor house in the 16th century but retains its 13th-century cloisters. At The Sign of The Angel is a delightful 15th-century inn, easily distinguished by being the only black and white building in the village. (Between Chippenham and Melksham on the A350.) (*Open March-October, tel 0249-73459.*)

Salisbury Cathedral

SALISBURY has been a prosperous Hampshire market town since the 13th century. Park your car in one of the large car parks on the edge of town and wander through the bustling town center to SALISBURY CATHEDRAL, the only ancient English cathedral built to a single design. Completed in 1258, it sits gracefully isolated from the busy town, surrounded by a large green field.

Britain's most famous ancient monument is STONEHENGE. Built over a period of almost 1000 years up to 1250 BC, this circular arrangement of towering stone slabs was probably meant either to mark the seasons or to be used as a symbol of worship. It is intriguing to ponder what prompted a society thousands of years ago to drag these immense stones many miles and erect them in just such a formation isolated in the middle of flat Salisbury Plain. Understandably, Stonehenge attracts many visitors. Your visit will be more enjoyable if you are prepared for coachloads of tourists. (On the A303 about 10 miles from Salisbury.) (*Open all year, tel 0272-734472.*)

When it is time to leave Bath take the A36 following signs for Bristol until you come to the A39 Wells road. WELLS is England's smallest cathedral city and the cathedral is glorious. Park you car in one of the well signposted car parks on the edge of town and walk through the bustling streets (*the market is on Wednesday*) to WELLS CATHEDRAL. The cathedral's west front is magnificently adorned with 400 statues of saints, angels, and prophets. The interior is lovely and on every hour the Great Clock comes alive as figures of four knights joust and one is unseated. From the cathedral you come to Vicars Close, a cobbled street of tall-chimneyed cottages with little cottage gardens built over 500 years ago as housing for the clerical community. On the other side of the cathedral regal swans swim lazily in the moat beneath the Bishop's Palace where at one time they rang a bell when they wanted to be fed but now visitors' picnics provide easier meals.

Nearby GLASTONBURY is a quiet market town steeped in legends. As the story goes, Joseph of Arimathea travelled here and leaned on his staff which rooted and flowered, a symbol that he should build a church. There may well have been a primitive church here but the ruins of GLASTONBURY ABBEY that you see are those of the enormous abbey complex that was begun in the 13th century and closed by Henry VIII just as it was completed. The abbey is in the center of town. Legend also has it that Glastonbury (at that time surrounded by marshes and lakes) was the Arthurian Isle of Avalon. Arthur and Guinevere are reputedly buried here and it is said that Arthur only sleeps and will arise when England needs him. (*Open all year, tel 0458-32267.*)

Cross the M5 near Bridgwater, detouring around the town, and follow the A39, Minehead road, to DUNSTER, a medieval town dominated by the battlements and towers of DUNSTER CASTLE (NT). Constructed by a Norman baron, it has been inhabited by the Luttrell family since 1376. While much of the castle was reconstructed in the last century, it has a superb staircase, halls, and dining room. (*Open all year, tel 0643-821314.*) Park before you enter the town and explore the shops and ancient buildings (including a dormered Yarn Market) of the High Street. On Mill Lane you can tour 18th-century DUNSTER WATERMILL (NT) that was restored to working order in 1979.

Continue your drive along the A39 watching for a sign that directs you to your right to the hamlet of SELWORTHY (NT). Its pretty green surrounded by elaborate thatched cottages makes this a very picturesque spot. The National Trust has a small visitors' center and excellent tea shop.

PORLOCK is a large bustling village with narrow streets. As the road bends down to the sea, the hamlet of PORLOCK WEIR appears as a few cottages and an old inn facing a tiny harbor dotted with boats.

A private toll road rises steeply out of Porlock Weir. It is a scenic, forested drive and the views looking back at Porlock Bay are spectacular. The toll road returns you to the A39 and the village of OARE, just a short distance to your left off the main road. R. D. Blackmore who wrote about the people, moods, and landscape of Exmoor used the little church at Oare for Lorna Doone's marriage to John Ridd and made Badgworthy Valley (a 3-mile walk away) the home of the cut-throat outlaw Doone family.

From Oare rounded, red mountains appear to drop dramatically down to the water's edge and a few black sand beaches. Soon the road dips down to the coast once more and reaches the neighboring villages of LYNTON and LYNMOUTH. The attractive Victorian Lynton which stands at the top of 500-foot cliffs and Lynmouth which nestles at its foot are joined together by a funky old cliff railway. Lynmouth is an old fishing village of old-style houses, some of which survived the 1952 flood when the river Lynn swept down the valley and through the town.

The road bends inland across the western stretches of Exmoor and south through BARNSTAPLE, a market center for the area. Continue along the A39 to BIDEFORD where a bridge sweeps you high above the old harbor.

Just beyond BUCKS CROSS you will see a small signpost for HOBBY DRIVE. This narrow coastal road winds through woodlands, provides panoramic views of CLOVELLY, and brings you out on the road above the village. Clovelly is an impossibly beautiful spot, its whitewashed cottages tumbling down cobblestone lanes to boats bobbing in the harbor far below. However, to be able to walk through this picturebook village you have to pass through a very commercial visitors' center, a real tourist trap.

Leave the A39 at the B3263 and detour on narrow country lanes leading to the picturesque little village of BOSCASTLE. Braced in a valley 400 feet above a little harbor, the town was named after the Boscastle family who once lived there, rather than an actual castle.

Nearby, TINTAGEL castle clings to a wild headland, exposed to coastal winds, claiming the honor of being King Arthur's legendary birthplace. The sea has cut deeply into the slate cliffs, isolating the castle. Climb the steep steps to the castle and gaze down at the sea far below. Prince Charles as Duke of Cornwall owns the castle, whose interior is more attractive than the exterior. The town itself, while it is quite touristy, has charm and the most adorable, and certainly most photographed, POST OFFICE (NT) in Britain.

Leaving Tintagel, follow signs for the A39, in the direction of Truro, to the A30 which takes you around Redruth, Cambourne, and Hayle to the A3074 to ST IVES, about a two-hour journey if the roads are not too crowded. St Ives is a former fishing town with cobbled streets and old cottages--it's very crowded in summer. With the decline of fishing came the artists who have done much to preserve its quaint cobbled streets and picturesque old cottages.

A most attractive stretch of Cornwall's coastline lies between St Ives and Land's End. Stone farm villages hug the bare expanse of land and are cooled by Atlantic Ocean breezes that wash up over the cliff edges. Abandoned old tin mine towers stand in ruins and regularly dot the horizon. On the northern outskirts of ST JUST is the GEEVOR TIN MINING MUSEUM. (*Open Easter-October, closed Saturdays.*)

The expression "from John O'Groats to Land's End" signifies the length of Britain from its northeasternmost point in Scotland to England's rocky promontory, Land's End, in the southwest. As the road rounds the peninsula from Land's End it is exposed to the calmer Channel waters. The powerful Atlantic surf, rolling and pounding long stretches of sandy beaches on one side, contrasts dramatically with the gentle tides that lap the shores of peaceful fishing ports on the other. Most visitors to Cornwall visit LAND'S END but be prepared to be disappointed: you have to walk through a compound of refreshment stands and exhibits to get to the viewpoint. An alternate, uncommercialized viewpoint is CAPE CORNWALL, reached from St Just.

Mount's Bay is just around the bend from Land's End. The pretty village of MOUSEHOLE (pronounced "mowzle") is tucked into a niche on its shores. With color-washed cottages crowded into a steep valley and multi-colored fishing boats moored at its feet, the village attracts a number of artists.

Pirates from France and the Barbary coast used to raid the flourishing port town of PENZANCE until the mid-18th century. Now it is a prosperous resort with a large harbor and beach.

The graceful sweep of Mount's Bay holds the island of ST MICHAEL'S MOUNT (NT). Its resemblance to the more famous mount in France is not coincidental, for it was founded by monks from Mont St Michel in 1044. A 19th-century castle and the ruins of the monastery crown the island which is reached at low tide on foot from the town of MARAZION. If you cannot coincide your arrival with low tide, do not worry--small boats ferry you the short distance to the island. The steep climb to the top of this fairytale mount is well worth the effort. (*Open daily April-October, limited winter opening, tel 0736-710507.*)

To the east lies FALMOUTH. Overlooking the holiday resort, yachting center, and ancient port are the ruins of PENDENNIS CASTLE. Built in 1540 to guard the harbor entrance, it was held during the Civil War by the Royalists and withstood six months of siege before being the last castle to surrender to Cromwell's troops in 1646. (*Open all year*) Falmouth is a bustling town whose narrow, shop-lined streets have a complex one-way system--parking is an additional problem. Unless you have shopping to do, avoid the congestion of the town center and follow signposts for Truro.

The road from Falmouth to St Mawes winds around the river estuary by way of TRURO. A faster and more scenic route is to take the KING HARRY FERRY across the river estuary. If you love wandering around gardens, you will enjoy TRELISSICK GARDENS (NT) filled with subtropical plants, located on the Falmouth side of the estuary. (*Open all year, tel 0872-865808.*)

ST MAWES is a charming, unspoilt fishing harbor at the head of the Roseland Peninsula. Its castle was built by Henry VIII to defend the estuary.

The 20 miles of coastline to the east of St Mawes hide several beautiful villages located down narrow, winding country lanes. PORTSCATHO is a lovely fishing village that has not been overrun with tourists. VERYAN is a quaint village where thatched circular houses were built so that "the devil had nowhere to hide." PORTLOE is a pretty fishing hamlet. The most easterly village is MEVAGISSEY whose beauty attracts writers, artists, and throngs of tourists.

Drive north through ST AUSTELL to LOSTWITHIEL, the 13th-century capital of Cornwall. Twenty miles to the east, LISKEARD is crowded in summer, but fortunately much of the traffic has been diverted around the town. Continue east about a 45-minute drive to the town of TAVISTOCK the western gateway to DARTMOOR NATIONAL PARK, a high, bleak moorland where sheep and ponies graze, rising to rocky peaks (tors) and dropping to picturesque wooded valleys. Below are some of the highlights of a visit to Dartmoor.

The view from atop HAYTOR CRAGS on the Bovey to Widecombe road is a spectacular one--there is a feel of *The Hound of the Baskervilles* to the place. Softer and prettier is the walk down wooded LYDFORD GORGE (NT) to White Lady Waterfall (between Tavistock and Okehampton.) (*Open all year, tel 082282-441.*) A cluster of cottages and a tall church steeple make up WIDECOMBE IN THE MOOR, the village made famous by the "Uncle Tom Cobbleigh" song: the famous fair is still held on the second Tuesday in September. The pretty town of CHAGFORD at the edge of the moor has attractive houses and hostelries grouped round the market square. BUCKLAND-IN-THE-MOOR is full of picturesque thatched cottages. BUCKLAND ABBEY (NT), a onetime Cistertian abbey and home of Sir Francis Drake, is now a museum with scale model ships from Drake's time to today amongst its exhibits. At BUCKFASTLEIGH you can take a steam train for 7 miles alongside the river Dart. Nearby is BUCKFAST ABBEY, famous for its tonic wine and colorful stained glass walls. CASTLE DROGO (NT) is a fanciful, castle-like home designed by Edward Lutyens overlooking the moor near Drewsteignton. (*Open all year, tel 0647-433306.*)

Leaving Dartmoor National Park, A roads quickly bring you to EXETER, a city that was much destroyed by German bombs in 1942. Happily the cathedral which was begun in 1260 survived. The old town towards the River Exe has many fine old buildings including the Custom House and a maze of little streets with old inns and quaint shops. On Town Quay is a fascinating MARITIME MUSEUM. (*Open all year, tel 0392-58075.*) The rebuilt center is a modern shopping complex.

From Exeter the M5 will connect you to all parts of Britain.

Southeast England

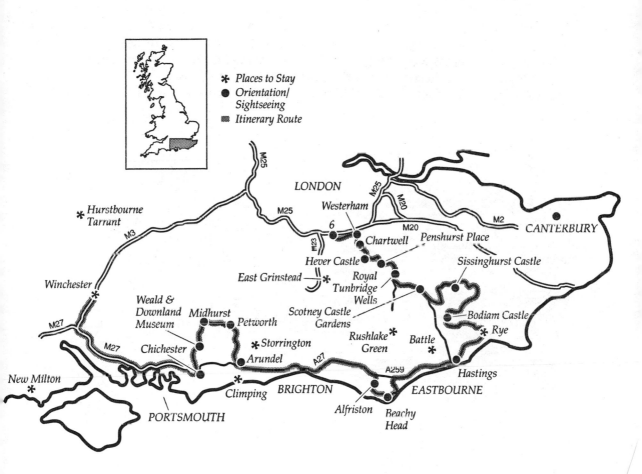

Places to Stay *

Orientation/Sightseeing ●

Itinerary Route ▦

LONDON

Hurstbourne Tarrunt *

M25

M3

M25

M23

6 ●

Westerham ●

Chartwell ●

Penshurst Place

M20

M20

M2

CANTERBURY ●

Hever Castle ●

Winchester *

East Grinstead *

Royal Tunbridge Wells ●

Sissinghurst Castle ●

M27

Weald & Downland Museum

Midhurst ●

Petworth ●

Scotney Castle Gardens

Bodiam Castle ●

M27

Chichester ●

Storrington *

Rushlake Green *

Battle *

Rye *

New Milton *

Arundel ●

A27

Hastings ●

Climping *

BRIGHTON

A259

EASTBOURNE

PORTSMOUTH

Alfriston

Beachy Head

33

Southeast England

Southeast from London through Kent and Sussex to England's southern coast, the land is fertile and the climate mild. Scores of narrow country lanes twist and turn among the gentle slopes of the pleasant countryside, leading you from Chartwell, Churchill's home, through castles, manors, and some of the most exquisitely beautiful gardens in England to Rye--full of history and rich in smugglers' tales. Along the busy, crowded coast you come to Brighton where seaside honky-tonk contrasts with the vivid spectacle of the onion domes of the Royal Pavilion, Arundel with its mighty fortress, and Portsmouth with its historic boats.

Scotney Castle Garden

CHARTWELL (NT), your first sightseeing destination, is signposted from exit 6 of the M25, through WESTERHAM and onto country lanes. Chartwell was the home of Winston Churchill from 1924 until his death in 1965, when Lady Churchill gave the house and its contents to the nation. To visit this large home and Churchill's studio full of his mementos and paintings is to have a glimpse into the family life of one of Britain's most famous politicians. (*Closed December, closed Mondays and Fridays, tel 0732-866368.*)

Leaving Chartwell, retrace your steps the short distance to the main road and follow signs for HEVER CASTLE, a small 13th-century moated castle that was at one time home to the Boleyn family. Anne Boleyn was Henry VIII's second wife and Elizabeth I's mother. At the turn of the century vast amounts of money were poured into the castle's restoration by William Waldorf Astor, an extremely wealthy American who forsook his native country and became a naturalized British citizen. Because the castle was far too small to provide accommodation for his family and friends Mr Astor built an adjacent village of snug, Tudor-style cottages and joined it to the castle. While the village is not open to the public, the restored castle, its rooms full of antiques that span the last 800 years, and the park-like grounds are open to the public. (*Open mid-March-November, tel 0732-865224.*)

Leave the castle to the left in the direction of Tunbridge Wells, turning left down a small country road to CHIDDINGSTONE, a National Trust village, whose short main street has several 16th- and 17th-century half-timbered houses, a church, and a tea shop. Park by the old houses and follow a footpath behind the cottages to the Chiding Stone, from which the village gets its name: nagging wives were brought here to be chided by the villagers.

Just beyond the village branch left at the oast house for Penshurst Station and PENSHURST PLACE, a 14th-century manor house with an Elizabethan front surrounded by magnificent parkland and gorgeous gardens. Here Sir Philip Sidney--poet, soldier, and statesman--was born and his descendant, Viscount de l'Isle, lives here today. The enormous, 14th-century great hall with its stone floor and lofty, ornate, beamed ceiling contrasts by its austerity with the sumptuously furnished state rooms. There is also a fascinating collection of old toys. The gardens are a delight, full of hedges and walls that divide them into flower-filled alleyways and rooms--each garden with a very different character. (*Open April-September, closed Mondays, tel 0892-870307.*)

ROYAL TUNBRIDGE WELLS lies 7 miles to the south. In its heyday Royal Tunbridge Wells rivaled Bath as a spa town. The Regency meeting place, The Pantiles, a terraced walk with shops behind a colonnade, is still there as are the elegant Regency parades and houses designed by Decimus Burton. Central parking is well signposted to the rear of the Corn Exchange which contains an exhibit, "Day at the Wells," which traces the town's growth from the time the spring water became fashionable for its curative powers to its popularity with wealthy Victorians.

Leave Royal Tunbridge Wells on the A267 following signposts for Eastbourne till you are directed to the left through BELLS YEW GREEN to cross the A21 (Hastings road) and enter SCOTNEY CASTLE GARDENS (NT), a gorgeous, romantic garden surrounding the moated ruins of a 14th-century castle. (*Open April-mid-November, closed Mondays and Tuesdays, tel 0892-890651.*)

Leave Scotney Castle Gardens to the left taking the A21 (Hastings road) for a short distance to FLIMWELL where you turn left on the A268 to HAWKSHURST and from here left on the A229 Maidstone road to CRANBROOK. While it is not necessary to go through Cranbrook to get to Sissinghurst Gardens, it makes a very worthwhile detour because it is a delightful town whose High Street has lots of lovely, white-board houses and shops, a fine medieval church, and a huge, white-board windmill with enormous sails. On the other side of town you come to the A262 where you turn right for the short drive to Sissinghurst Castle Gardens.

SISSINGHURST CASTLE (NT) was a gaol for 3,000 French prisoners in the Seven Years War. Its ruined remains were bought by Vita Sackville-West and her husband Harold Nicolson in 1930 and together they created the most gorgeous gardens with areas divided off like rooms and each room a distinctly different, beautiful garden. They also rescued part of the derelict castle where you can climb the tower in which Vita wrote her books. At the entrance to the garden an old barn has been tastefully converted into a tearoom and shop. (*Open March-October, closed Mondays, tel 0580-712850.*)

Continue along the A262 to BIDDENDEN and take the A28 through TENTERDEN with its broad High street of tiled and weather-boarded houses to the A268 (Hawkshurst road) where you turn right for the short drive to the village of SANDHURST. Here you turn left onto country lanes to BODIAM CASTLE (NT), a small, picturesque, squat fortress with crenelated turrets surrounded by a wide moat and pastoral countryside. Richard II ordered the castle built as a defensive position to secure the upper reaches of the Rother against French raiders who had ravaged nearby towns. But an attack never came. (*Open all year, tel 0580-830436.*)

Turn left as you leave the castle following a country lane to STAPLE CROSS where you turn left on the B2165 which brings you into RYE, a fortified seaport that was often attacked by French raiders. However, the sea has long since retreated, leaving the town marooned almost 2 miles inland. Find the quaintest street in Rye, Mermaid Street, with its weatherboard and tile-hung houses and up one cobblestoned block you find yourself on the doorstep of The Mermaid Inn. Opened in 1420, THE MERMAID INN is a fascinating relic of the past. As late as Georgian days, smugglers frequented this strikingly timbered inn and used to sit drinking in the pub with their pistols on the table, unchallenged by the law. Near the Norman Church is the 13th-century YPRES TOWER--formerly a castle and prison, it is now a museum of local history. LAMB HOUSE (NT) (on West Street near the church) was the home of American novelist Henry James from 1898 to 1916. To learn more about Rye's fascinating history attend the sound and light show at the RYE TOWN MODEL. (*Open April-October, tel 0797-223254.*)

Rye

Leave Rye on the A259 taking this fast road around HASTINGS and BEXHILL to EASTBOURNE where you follow signs for the seafront of this old-fashioned holiday resort and continue onto the B2103 which brings you up and onto the vast chalk promontory, BEACHY HEAD, that rises above the town. It is a glorious, windswept place of soaring seagulls and springy turf that abruptly ends as the earth drops away to giant chalk cliffs that plummet into the foaming sea. This is the starting point for the South Downs Way, a walking path. Passing the Belle Tout lighthouse, you come to Birling Gap, a beach once popular with smugglers but now favored by bathers. The most dramatic scenery, the Seven Sisters, giant, white, windswept cliffs, are an envigorating walk from the tiny village of FRISTON.

From Friston take the A259 to WESTDEAN where you turn right for

ALFRISTON, an adorable village on the South Downs Way that traces its origins back to Saxon times.   Behind the main village street in a little cottage garden facing the village green sits the CLERGY HOUSE (NT) with its deep thatch roof, the first building acquired by the National Trust, in 1896.

Either the fast A27 or the slower coastal road (A259) will bring you into BRIGHTON, a onetime sleepy fishing village that was transformed into a fashionable resort at the beginning of the 19th century by the Prince Regent building his fanciful, extravagant ROYAL PAVILION with its onion domes and gaudy paintwork.   Follow signs for the town center and park near the pavilion, an extravaganza of a place full of colorful, rather overpowering decor.   (*Open all year, tel 0273-603005.*)

Nearby are THE LANES, narrow streets of former fishermen's cottages now filled with restaurants, and antique and gift shops.   The seafront is lined by a 3-mile-long promenade with the beach below and gardens and tall terraces above.   Many of the once fashionable townhouses are now boarding houses and small hotels but this does not detract from the old-fashioned seaside atmosphere of the town. Stretching out into the sea, the white, wooden Palace Pier harks back to an earlier age.   At the end is a delightful, old-fashioned funfair with a helter-skelter and carousel horses along with other rides.

Leave Brighton along the seafront in the direction of Hove to join the A27 at Shoreham-by-Sea.   This section of the A27 passes through suburb after suburb and is the least interesting part of this itinerary.   On the outskirts of ARUNDEL the massive keep and towers of ARUNDEL CASTLE rise above the town.   Built just after the Norman Conquest to protect this area from sea pirates and raiders, the castle contains a collection of armor, tapestries, and other interesting artifacts. (*Open April-October, closed Saturdays, tel 0903-882173.*)

From Arundel take the A284 inland towards Pulborough and then follow signs through the narrow, winding old streets of PETWORTH, where several of the shops are antique stores, to PETWORTH HOUSE (NT), an enormous, 17th-century house in a vast deer park with landscaping by Capability Brown. The house, completed by the 6th Duke of Somerset in 1696, retains the 13th-century chapel of an earlier mansion and houses a proud art collection which includes a series of landscapes by Turner and also paintings by Holbein, Rembrandt, Van Dyck, Gainsborough, Titian, Rubens, and Reynolds. (*Open April-October, closed Mondays and Fridays, tel 0798-42207.*)

Retrace your route the short distance into Petworth and take the A272 through MIDHURST to take the A286 (Chichester road). Midhurst has some fine old houses and attractive inns. Knockhundred Row leads from North Street to Red Lion Street and the old timbered market. Curfew is faithfully rung each evening at 8 pm in the parish church. Legend has it that a rider, lost in darkness, followed the sound of the church bells and found his way to the town. To show his gratitude he purchased a piece of land in Midhurst, now called Curfew Garden, which was presented to the town as a gift and made money available for the nightly ringing of the bells.

Across the South Downs the A286 brings you to the WEALD AND DOWNLAND MUSEUM, an assortment of old, humble buildings such as farmhouses and barns brought to and restored on this site after their loss to demolition was inevitable. Within several of the buildings are displays showing the development of buildings through the ages. (*Open March-October, tel 024363-348.*)

Leaving the museum, take the A286 around Chichester to the A27 Portsmouth road which leads you onto the M275 to the historic center of PORTSMOUTH and your goal, the *HMS VICTORY* and *MARY ROSE*. The *HMS Victory*, Nelson's flagship at the Battle of Trafalgar in 1805, has been restored and kitted out to show what life was like on board. Nearby the *Mary Rose*, Henry VIII's flagship, is housed in a humidified building that preserves its remains which were raised from the seabed several years ago. The Navy Museum has a display of model ships, figureheads, and a panorama depicting the Battle of Trafalgar. (*Open all year, tel 0705-812931.*)

Retrace your steps up the M275 and onto the M27 which quickly brings you to the A33/M3 and WINCHESTER where a magnificent cathedral stands at the center of the city. Park in one of the car parks on the edge of town and walk into the pedestrian heart of the city that was the capital of England in King Alfred's reign during the 9th century and stayed so for 200 years. The 556-foot-long cathedral was started in 1079 and finished in 1404. Treasures include a memorial window to Izaak Walton, a black marble font, seven chancery chapels for special masses, medieval wall paintings, stained glass, and tombs of ancient kings including King Canute. More Winchester memorabilia and lodging, good food, and ale can be enjoyed at the nearby WYKEMAN ARMS. Close by is Winchester College, founded in 1382, one of the oldest public schools in England. Its motto is "Manners Makyth Man."

Leaving Winchester, the M3 will quickly take you back to London.

Cambridge & East Anglia

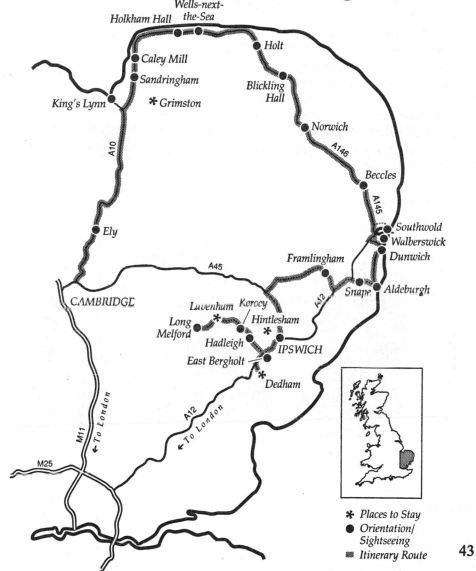

Holkham Hall

Wells-next-the-Sea

Caley Mill

Sandringham

King's Lynn

* Grimston

Holt

Blickling Hall

Norwich

A146

Beccles

A145

Southwold

Walberswick

Dunwich

A10

Ely

A45

Framlingham

A12

Snape

Aldeburgh

CAMBRIDGE

Lavenham

Kersey

* Hintlesham

Long Melford

*

Hadleigh

IPSWICH

East Bergholt

* Dedham

M11

To London

A12

To London

M25

43

* Places to Stay
● Orientation/Sightseeing
▓ Itinerary Route

Cambridge & East Anglia

Many visit the famous university town of Cambridge, but few travellers venture beyond to explore the bulge of England's eastern coastline with its sky-wide landscapes, stunning sunsets, lofty windmills, and unspoilt villages. This itinerary takes you from the vast fenlands, drained by the Dutch in the 17th century, along the pancake-flat Norfolk coastline with the sea often just out of sight beyond fields and marshes, into Norwich with its ancient streets and vast cathedral, through sleepy Suffolk villages full of quaint cottages to "Constable Country" where John Constable painted so many of his famous paintings. Be sure to visit Cambridge, but expand your trip to explore this quiet corner of Britain.

Kersey

Leaving London, navigate yourself onto the M11 for the fast, two-hour drive to CAMBRIDGE, a city that contains much new building but at whose heart is a fascinating university complex whose history spans over 700 years. Park your car in one of the well marked car parks near the town center, buy a guidebook and set out to explore, for this is a city for strolling and browsing.

At most times visitors can go into college courtyards, chapels, dining halls, and certain gardens. KING'S COLLEGE CHAPEL is one of the finest buildings in England, with Rubens' masterpiece, the "Adoration of the Magi," framing the altar. Be sure not to miss CLARE COLLEGE, TRINITY COLLEGE, and ST JOHN'S COLLEGE, which backs onto the enclosed stone "Bridge of Sighs." Explore the various alleys and streets on foot, row, or punt, drifting under the willow trees that line the River Cam. Boats are for hire at Silver Street Bridge and Quayside.

Leaving Cambridge on the A10 towards ELY, you soon come to open countryside offering sky-wide horizons of flat farmland that are soon punctuated by the soaring mass of ELY CATHEDRAL, a building so large that it seems to dwarf the little market town that surrounds it. Until the surrounding fens were drained, Ely was an island, surrounded by water, and the cathedral must have appeared even more magnificent than it does today. This awesome structure was built in 1083, awesome not only for its sheer size but because it is an amazing piece of engineering, its huge tower held up by eight massive oak timbers each more than 60 feet in length.

Leaving Ely, regain the A10 following it around Downham Market to KING'S LYNN, a large, bustling town with a well marked historic core. A market is held every Saturday and Tuesday and the port has many fine old buildings: the Guildhall (1421), the Customs House (1683), and St Margaret's church. George Vancouver's father was a customs officer hereabouts. He set sail for the north coast of Western America (1790) and the Canadian city and island are named for him.

Leaving King's Lynn, follow signs for the A149 in the direction of Hunstanton. After several miles turn right for SANDRINGHAM, one of the Royal Family's homes, and almost immediately first left to take you on a scenic drive through the woodlands that surround it. This huge Victorian house was bought in 1861 by Edward VII, at that time Prince of Wales, because he did not like Osborne House on the Isle of Wight. From mid-April to the end of September on Sunday, Monday, Tuesday, Wednesday, and Thursday from 11 am several rooms in the house and the grounds are open to the public--provided that the Royal Family is not in residence. (*Tel 0553-772675.*)

Leave the car park to your left, passing the main gates (the Norwich gates, a wedding gift to Edward from the city of Norwich) and left through Dersingham to regain the A149. In summer the air is heavy with the scent of lavender and the fields surrounding CALEY MILL are a brilliant purple for this is one of the country's centers for the cultivation of lavender. There is a gift shop selling every imaginable lavender product.

After bypassing Hunstanton, the A149 becomes narrower, pottering along through attractive villages of pebble and red-brick cottages (Thornham, Titchwell, Brancaster Staithe, and Overy Staithe) as it traces the flat Norfolk coast with the sea often just out of sight beyond fields and marshes. This is not a coastline of dramatic cliffs and headlands--the land merely ends and the sea begins.

On the outskirts of HOLKHAM you follow the wall surrounding HOLKHAM HALL to its driveway. This magnificent, 18th-century Palladian mansion, the seat of the "modern" Earls of Leicester, contains paintings by Rubens, Van Dyck, Poussin, and Gainsborough; 17th- and 18th-century tapestry and furniture; thousands of items of bygone days, such as steam engines, kitchen equipment, smithy tools, ploughs, and fire engines; and Greek and Roman statuary. (*Open June-September, closed Fridays and Saturdays, tel 0328-710227.*) Detour into WELLS-NEXT-THE-SEA, one of the few villages along this coast to have a waterfront.

Leave the coast behind and turn inland following the B1156 through Holt in the direction of Norwich to BLICKLING HALL (NT), a grand, 17th-century red-brick house set in acres of parkland. The house if full of fine pictures, tapestries, and gracious furniture. (*Open April-October, closed Mondays and Thursdays, tel 0263-733084.*)

Following signs for Norwich, join the A140 which takes you to the heart of this sprawling city. NORWICH is rich in historic treasures including a beautiful Norman cathedral, topped by a 15th-century spire, with a huge close running down to the River Wensum. The castle, built by one of William the Conqueror's supporters, is now the CASTLE MUSEUM. (*Open all year, closed Sundays, tel 0603-223624.*) STRANGERS HALL, a 14th-century home, has its rooms furnished in the styles of different periods. Elm Hill is a cobbled street with shops and houses from the 14th to the 18th century. COLMAN'S MUSTARD SHOP in Bridewell Alley is a major tourist attraction. Norwich has an interesting fruit and vegetable market (*closed Sunday*) and some very nice shops and restaurants.

From the ring road surrounding Norwich take the A146 in the direction of Lowestoft, turning on the A145 through Beccles to the A12 where you turn left and first right on the A1095 into SOUTHWOLD, a quiet, sedate Victorian/Edwardian seaside resort, with its most attractive houses lining the seafront and its narrow rows of shops forming the town center. Across the river estuary lies WALBERSWICK, a pretty little fishing/holiday village of cottages and a pub, reached by a little ferry that plies back and forth (or the longer road route that traces the estuary).

Regaining the A12, turn left, towards Ipswich, for a short distance to the village of BLYTHBURGH to visit its church which is so imposing in size that hereabouts it is referred to as Blythburgh Cathedral. The size of the church is indicative of the community's importance in years gone by when it was a thriving port, with its own mint on the estuary of the River Blyth. Its prosperity declined and the church was neglected until it was restored this century. Carvings of the Seven Deadly Sins decorate the pew-ends and the rare, wooden Jack-o'-the-Clock.

A short distance farther along the A12 brings you to the left-hand turn for DUNWICH--cross the heathlands and go through the village to the car park in front of the Flora Tea Rooms which serves excellent fish and chips, tea, and coffee beneath the pebbly bank that separates it from the sea. The fish comes fresh from the fishermen who draw their boats up on the beach. Along the headlands lie the few remains of the medieval port of Dunwich which was almost completely swept out to sea in 1326 by a great storm. What was left has continued to be eroded by the sea. Local legend has it that before a storm the bells of Dunwich's 15 submerged churches can be heard ringing.

A short drive brings you to MINSMERE NATURE RESERVE, a celebrated place for birdwatching, and through WESTLETON to ALDEBURGH, a charming town whose streets are lined with Georgian houses and whose High Street has antique and other interesting shops. The local council still meets in the half-timbered Moot Hall (1512). Benjamin Britten, who directed the Aldeburgh music festival for 30 years until his death in 1976, based his opera *Peter Grimes* on a poem by local poet George Crabbe.

Head inland on the A1094 turning left onto the B1069 into SNAPE to arrive at SNAPE MALTINGS, a collection of red-brick granaries and old malthouses that has been converted into a riverside center with interesting garden and craft shops, art galleries, tea rooms, and a concert hall, home of the Aldeburgh music festival every June. From here you can take a boat trip on the River Alde which meanders through the marshes to the sea.

Continue inland and map a quiet country route through sleepy Suffolk villages and rolling farmland to FRAMLINGHAM, a quiet market town where Mary Tudor was proclaimed queen of England in 1553. The town is dominated by a 12th-century castle with tall, gray-stone walls linking its towers. (*Open Easter-September, tel 0728-723330.*)

Two miles away at SAXTEAD GREEN a 200-year-old Post Mill, one of Suffolk's few remaining windmills, stands guard over the green. (*Open April-September, closed Sundays.*)

From Saxtead Green follow the A1120 towards Ipswich and the A45 as it skirts Ipswich and joins the A12 (direction Colchester) at a large roundabout (it is busy dual carriageways like these that keep the small roads quiet and peaceful). Leave the A12 at the third exit following signs to your left for DEDHAM, a pretty village settled along the banks of the lazy River Stour which was made famous by John Constable who painted its mill and church spire on several occasions. (Even though it is just a river bend away from East Bergholt, Constable's birthplace, today you have to go between the two villages by way of the busy A12.) Sir Alfred Munnings, the painter of horses, lived in Castle House which is now a museum containing examples of his work.

Retrace your steps to the A12 and return in the direction of Ipswich following signs for FLATFORD and EAST BERGHOLT where John Constable was born in 1776, the son of the miller of Flatford Mill. The little hamlet of Flatford, now a National Trust property, is signposted in East Bergholt. A one-way lane directs you to the car park above the hamlet (it is not well signposted and you may have to stop and ask). The collection of cottages has been restored to the way it was in Constable's time and a tearoom serves scrumptious afternoon teas and sandwiches. If the weather is fine, you can take a picnic, hire a rowing boat, and while away an afternoon on the river. The National Trust shop sells a packet which includes a map that identifies where Constable painted some of his most famous pictures and postcards of the paintings so you can wander along the river bank and pinpoint the very spot where he painted his father's mill, Willy Lott's cottage, or the boatbuilders at work. The scene has changed little since those times--apart from the tourists. Constable said of the area, "Those scenes made me a painter." (*Open April-October, tel 0206-298260.*)

Leaving the Constable complex, the road returns you to East Bergholt where you turn right to go through the village and take the B1070 to HADLEIGH, a large market town whose High Street has some lovely old houses. On the edge of the town cross the A1071 and then take the first left and first right to bring you onto the main street of KERSEY, the most picture-book perfect of all Suffolk villages, whose narrow main street is lined with ancient weavers' cottages, grand merchants' houses, and old pubs, each jostling one another for roadside space and each colorwashed a different color. In the middle of the village a stream runs across the road and drivers must take care to avoid the village ducks.

Regain the A1141 and a short drive brings you through MONKS ELEIGH with its thatched cottages and large craft shop selling traditional corn dollies to LAVENHAM which in Tudor times was one of England's wealthiest towns. Now it is a sleepy village where leaning timbered houses line its quiet street and continue into the market square with its 16th-century cross and LAVENHAM GUILDHALL (NT) which houses displays of local history and the medieval wool industry. (*Open April-October, tel 0787-247646.*) If you are captivated by the serenity of Lavenham, morning coffee or afternoon tea at the lovely Swan Hotel serve as a pleasurable excuse to linger.

Country lanes take you across country the 5 miles to LONG MELFORD whose long, broad, tree-lined main street houses many antique shops and leads to the village green which is overshadowed by the magnificent, 15th-century Holy Trinity Church. A short walk away the red-brick, turreted MELFORD HALL (NT) contains a wealth of porcelain, paintings, and antiques and a display of Beatrix Potter's paintings--she was a frequent visitor here. (*Open May-October, closed Mondays, Tuesdays, and Fridays, tel 0787-880286.*)

Leaving Long Melford, you can go south to the A12 or east to the M11 which quickly return you to London.

Derbyshire Dales & Villages

SHEFFIELD

Edale
Castleton
A625
Hope
Hathersage
A623
Eyam
Tideswell
Ashford-in-the-Water
Baslow
Buxton
A6
Chatsworth
Chesterfield
A619
Bakewell
Haddon Hall
A515
Monyash &
Arbor Low
Rowsley
Parsley
Hay
Hartington
Matlock
A515
Alstonfield
Dovedale
Ilam
Tissington
Ashbourne

* Places to Stay
● Orientation/
   Sightseeing
▓ Itinerary Route

51

Derbyshire Dales & Villages

Every structure in this itinerary--manor houses, churches, cottages, farmhouses, shops--even the walls that trim the fields making a patchwork of the landscape--is built of gray stone.   This is the Peak District, a National Park, where you can enjoy the beauty of a wild landscape of rolling rocky pastures, sheltered valleys, and windswept moors laced by swift rivers tumbling through deep dales--Monks Dale, Monsal Dale, Miller Dale, and, the most beautiful of all, Dovedale where the River Dove flows through a rocky, wooded ravine and is crossed by stepping stones. While this is a driving itinerary, to really appreciate the wild beauty of this area you have to foresake your car and proceed on foot--on the miles of well marked footpaths--or rent a bike and pedal the cycle routes that travel disused railway lines and quiet country lanes.

Castleton

This itinerary begins in ASHBOURNE, a small market town just south of the Peak District National Park where on Thursdays and Saturdays market stalls crowd the town square. Close by, on St John Street, visit the Gingerbread Shop which sells aromatic Ashbourne gingerbread and baked goods from a restored 15th-century timber-framed shop that gives you a glimpse of how beautiful Ashbourne must have been during its heyday. (*Cycle hire for the Tissington Trail is Ashbourne Cycle Hire, Mapleton Lane, Ashbourne, Derbyshire, tel 0335-43156.*)

Leave Ashbourne on the A515, Buxton road, and watch for a discreetly signposted right-hand turn which brings you through a broad avenue of trees to TISSINGTON with its Jacobean manor house, Norman church, limestone cottages, and ducks swimming on the village pond. Tissington is reputedly the birthplace of the Derbyshire village tradition of well dressing, giving thanks for the unfailing supply of fresh water that the village wells provided by creating intricate, large mosaic pictures from flower petals and placing them beside the village wells. These spectacular displays are very interesting to visit, so in the course of this itinerary, the dates that villages dress their wells is mentioned in parentheses, for example, "TISSINGTON *(wells dressed for Ascension day)*." If you carry on through the village and across open farmland you come to a ford where the road splashes through a brook.

Retrace your steps to the A515 and cross it, heading through THORPE village and down into DOVEDALE. Dr Johnston gave it a glowing testimonial: "He who has seen Dovedale has no need to visit the Highlands." Cars can go no farther than the car park from whence you walk into the dale, crossing the River Dove on stepping stones and entering a rocky ravine. The farther you walk into the dale the more you are tempted to continue as round each river bend beautiful scenery unfolds--fantastic rock formations, steeply wooded hillsides, and the noisy tumbling water. The length of the dale is a delightful, 4-mile walk. Walkers can be dropped at the car park and picked up in Milldale by Viators Bridge.

At a bend in the road is ILAM (pronounced I lamb), a picture-postcard estate village, built to house the workers on what was once a shipping magnate's vast holdings. On to ALSTONFIELD (pronounced Alstonfeld) and the Post Office Tea Shop which serves scrumptious scones and cream. (Turn right here if you are picking walkers up in nearby Milldale.)

Well Dressing

It is a short drive into HARTINGTON (*wells dressed on second Saturday in September*) with its white limestone cottages, shops, and pubs. Admire the mallards waddling by the village pond and visit the cheese shop, an outlet for the last of Derbyshire's cheese factories producing Hartington Stilton and Buxton Blue.

Leave Hartington on the B5054, Ashbourne road, and take the first left, signposted Crowdicote, following the narrow dale. As the dale widens, turn right to

PARSLEY HAY (*Parsley Hay Cycle Hire, Parsley Hay near Buxton, Derbyshire, tel 0298-84493*). From here you can cycle the Tissington Trail towards Ashbourne or the High Peak Trail to Cromford. At the main road turn left (towards Buxton) and immediately right towards Monyash then right again following discreet signposts for ARBOR LOW, Derbyshire's answer to Stonehenge, except that the huge monoliths have all fallen to the ground and you will probably be the only visitors. The stones are set atop a bare hill, swept by cold winds, and reached by tramping across fields from a lonely farm. Pause and wonder why man 4,000 years ago built here.

Retrace your path to the MONYASH road, turning right in the village onto the B5055 which leads you into BAKEWELL *(wells dressed on last Saturday in June)*, a lovely market town ringed by wooded hills where a picturesque, 700-year-old arched and buttressed bridge spans the swiftly flowing River Wye. The Tourist Information Centre in the splendid, 17th-century market hall has displays on the Peak District and information pamphlets. Behind it are set the market stalls where every Monday a farmers' market is held--offering everything from lengths of dress fabric to underwear and pigs. You can buy the original Bakewell tarts (known as puddings in Bakewell) from Ye Olde Original Pudding Shop and the splendid new Bakewell Pudding Factory on Granby Arcade. The town has some excellent shops (china, antique, clothing, and hardware). Up the hill, just behind the church, is The Old House Museum, a folk museum, displaying kitchen and farm equipment (*Open April-October, tel 0629-81347.*)

Three miles along the A6 in the direction of Matlock lies HADDON HALL, a 14th-century manor, home of the Duke of Rutland. This house is more interesting to tour than the opulent Chatsworth House (which is your next stop) because it lacks the vastness and grandeur of Chatsworth and you can really imagine that people actually lived in these aged rooms hung with threadbare tapestries and decorated with magnificent woodcarvings. Parts of the chapel walls are covered with barely discernible frescos that date back to the 11th century. In summer the gardens are a fragrant haven with a profusion of climbing roses and clematis decorating the house and the stone walls of the terraces. (*Open April-September, tel 0629-812855.*)

Continue along the A6 to ROWSLEY where you can tour Caudwell's Mill, a water-powered flour mill, and visit the craft shops. Leaving Rowsley, take the first left (B6012). Pass the edge of BEELEY, cross the River Derwent on a narrow humpbacked bridge, and enter the vast Chatsworth estate. (Immediately on your left is the Chatsworth Garden Centre which, in addition to a vast array of all things garden, has a gift and coffee shop.) The road leads you through rolling green parkland to CHATSWORTH HOUSE, the enormous (the roof covers 1.3 acres) home of the Duke and Duchess of Devonshire. While the Duke and Duchess occupy a portion of the house, you can walk through the opulent halls admiring priceless paintings, furnishings, silver plate, and china. Best of all, though, are the acres and acres of landscaped gardens with the great fountain playing and the lawns above the house, laid down in 1760 and groomed ever since (except in wartime). The tea shop is a must. If you are travelling with children, they will enjoy a visit to the farm and the adventure playground. (*Open April-October, tel 0246-582204.*)

The picturesque village of EDENSOR (pronounced Ensor), mentioned in the Doomsday Book of 1086, was much rebuilt and moved here in the 19th century by a Duke who did not want to see it from his park. Kathleen Kennedy, JFK's sister, lies buried near the handsome old church.

Leave the estate in the direction of Baslow and take the first left, B6048, to PILSEY where the farm shop sells an interesting variety of nifty gifts and produce from the Chatsworth estate. As the B6048 merges with the main road take the first right on the A6020 (Ashford) following it to ASHFORD-IN-THE-WATER and cross the river into this picturesque village strung along the River Wye. "Sheepwash" is the oldest and quaintest of the village's bridges. Built for packhorses and now closed to traffic, it gets its name from the adjacent stone enclosure in which sheep used to be washed.

Chatsworth House

Follow the narrow lanes upwards to MONSAL HEAD where the ground seemingly falls away and opens up to a magnificent vista of the River Wye running through MONSAL DALE. Go straight across, beside the Monsal Head car park, and follow the road as it winds down into and along the dale to Cressbrook mill, where the road climbs steeply past the terraces of mill cottages clinging precariously to the hillsides. The first terrace is where pauper apprentices lived and higher up are the more opulent foremen's houses. Emerging from the dale, the narrow road skirts stone walled fields to LITTON *(wells dressed in June)*, a delightful stone village round a green where you turn left for Tideswell.

The magnificent, spacious, 14th-century church at TIDESWELL *(wells dressed on*

Saturday nearest John the Baptist day, June 24th) is so impressive that it is often described as "the cathedral of the Peak." It was built between 1300 and 1370 when Tideswell was an affluent place and it is fortunate that Tideswell fell upon hard times so that parishioners could not afford to update their church as ecclesiastical fashions changed.

Leaving Tideswell, you come to the A623 and turn left in the direction of Chapel en le Frith to SPARROWPIT where you turn right at the Wanted Inn. Passing an enormous quarry, you see that half the mountain is missing--gone to build all the lovely stone houses and cottages. When you come to a brown and white country sign stating "Castleton Caverns, Peveril Castle, light traffic only," turn right into Winnats Pass which drops you down a steep ravine between high limestone cliffs.

As the ravine opens up to the valley, SPEEDWELL CAVERN presents itself. This is one of several famous caverns (mixtures of natural cavities and lead mine workings resplendent with stalagmites and stalactites) found around Castleton. Speedwell differs from the other caverns in that it is reached by a 105-step descent to a motor-boat which takes you along an underground canal to a cavern which was the working face of the former Speedwell Mine where Blue John, a translucent blue variety of fluorspar, found only in this area, was mined. (*Open all year, tel 0433-20512.*)

Before you head off to explore other nearby caves (Blue John, Treak Cliff, and Peak), head into CASTLETON, a village huddled far below the brooding ruins of PEVERIL CASTLE where Henry II accepted the submission of Malcolm of Scotland in 1157. Henry had the keep built in 1176, while other parts were added in later years. (*Open all year.*)

Below the castle is the huge mouth of PEAK CAVERN, an enormous cave that once sheltered ropemakers' cottages. The soot from the chimneys of this subterranean village can be seen on the cave's roof. Regrettably, the entrance to the cave has been marred by the erection of a high wooden barrier giving access to the cave only to those willing to pay an entrance fee. In the narrow village's streets you will find cafes and pubs and several shops selling the polished Blue John set into bracelets, rings, and the like.

This is walking country and you might consider walking up MAM TOR (the big bulky mountain beside Winnets Pass) known hereabouts as "Shivering Mountain" because its layers of soft shale set between harder beds of rock are constantly crumbling. Those in search of a longer walk may wish to go to nearby EDALE where the Pennine Way starts its 250-mile path north.

Leave Castleton on the A625 travelling along the broad Hope valley through HOPE *(wells dressed last Saturday in June)* and BAMFORD to HATHERSAGE, a thriving, non-traditional Derbyshire village strung out along the main road. Its tourist attractions center on its 14th-century church, St Michael and All Angels, built by a knight named Robert Eyre. Memorial brasses to the Eyre family are in the church and Charlotte Bronte used the village as "Morton" in *Jane Eyre*. In the graveyard is the reputed grave of Little John, the friend and lieutenant of Robin Hood.

Leaving the churchyard, backtrack on the A625 for a short distance, taking the first left (B6001), signposted Bakewell, beyond the village where you turn right, opposite The Plough, up a narrow country lane signposted "Gliding Club." This country lane takes you through the hamlet of ABNEY past the gliding club and the historic Barrel Inn (offering views of the valley, good pub food, and refreshing ale) and brings you into EYAM (pronounced Eem) *(wells dressed last Saturday in August)*.

This large mining and quarrying village was made famous by its self-imposed quarantine when plague hit the village in 1665. It was thought that the virus arrived in a box of cloth from London brought by a visiting tailor. The rector persuaded the community to quarantine themselves to prevent the plague spreading to outlying villages and for over a year the village was supplied by neighboring villagers who left food and supplies at outlying points. 259 people from 76 families perished. Little plaques on Eyam's cottages give the names of the victims who lived there; the church has a plague register and just inside the door is the letter written by the young rector when his wife succumbed (Katherine Mompesson is buried near the Saxon cross in the churchyard). The most poignant reminder of these grim days lies in a field about 1/2 mile from the village where within a solitary little enclosure, known as the Riley Graves, are the memorials to a father and his six children, all of whom died within eight days of each other.

Leave Eyam in the direction of Bakewell, travelling down a steeply wooded gorge which brings you to the A623. Following signs for Chesterfield, you drive down narrow Middleton Dale whose limestone cliffs are so sheer they almost block the sunlight from the road to STONEY MIDDLETON, an appropriately named village huddling beneath the cliffs. It does not look at all inviting from the main road but its quiet side streets and pretty church are full of character.

Driving a few miles farther along the A623 brings you to the winding lanes of BASLOW where the River Derwent flows past tidy houses on the northern edge of the Chatsworth estate. From here fast roads will bring you to CHESTERFIELD (visit the leaning spire and if it is a Monday, Friday, or Saturday, you will enjoy the interesting open-air market) where you can join the M1 at junction 29.

North Yorkshire

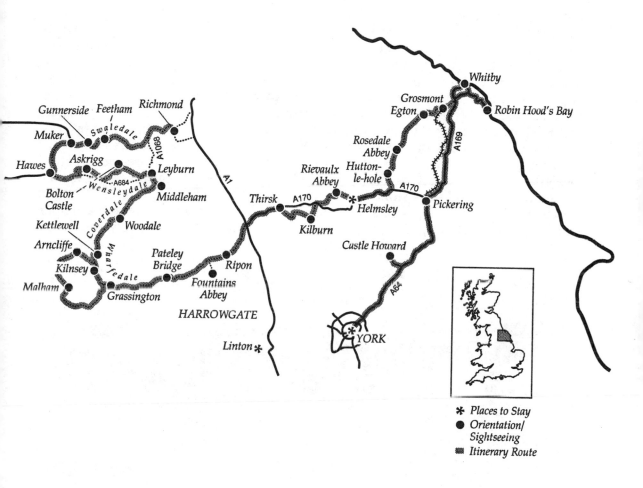

Gunnerside Feetham Richmond

Muker Swaledale A1068

Hawes Askrigg Leyburn

A684

Bolton Wensleydale Middleham
Castle

Kettlewell Coverdale Woodale

Arncliffe Wharfedale

Kilnsey Pateley Ripon
Bridge

Malham Fountains
Grassington Abbey

HARROWGATE

Linton *

A1

Thirsk A170

Kilburn

Castle Howard

A64

YORK

Rievaulx
Abbey

Rosedale
Abbey Hutton-
le-hole

Helmsley Pickering

A170

Grosmont
Egton

A169

Whitby

Robin Hood's Bay

* Places to Stay
● Orientation/
  Sightseeing
▧ Itinerary Route

61

North Yorkshire

After exploring historic York, this itinerary samples the wild and beautiful countryside of two National Parks: the North York Moors and the Yorkshire Dales. This is an area of rugged, untamed, harsh beauty in its landscape and its stout stone villages. With seemingly endless miles of heather-covered moorlands, few roads, and even fewer sturdy villages sheltering in green valleys, the North York Moors appears vast and untamed, dipping to the sea to embrace the villages and towns of the east coast. While across the flat expanse of the Vale of York lie the Yorkshire Dales, characterized by sleepy rivers weaving through peaceful valleys and by gray-stone walls bounding the fields and tracing patterns on the countryside to the moorlands above. Here every valley has a name and a very different character-- Swaledale, Littondale, Coverdale, and Wharfedale. And scattered throughout Yorkshire are small gray-stoned villages with a cluster of stone houses, a hump-backed bridge, a friendly pub, and an ancient church. Yorkshire people are open and hospitable, offering one of England's most genuine and friendly welcomes.

If you delight in historic towns you will love YORK, a compact city brimful of history encircled by 700-year-old walls with great imposing gates known as "bars." There has been a settlement here since Roman times and by the time of the Norman Conquest it was, after London, the principal city of England.

Your first stop in York should be the Tourist Information Centre on St Leonards, near Bootham Bar. Avail yourself of a detailed city map and ask about walking tours that will, in the space of several hours, orient you to this historic city.

Walk the narrow, cobblestoned streets with such appealing names as The Shambles, Stonegate, and Goodramgate past timbered buildings whose upper stories lean out, almost forming a bridge over the streets. While interesting shops abound, the National Trust Shop on Goodramgate and Betty's Bakery and Tearooms on St Helen's Square are ones to target.

York's magnificent cathedral is known simply as THE MINSTER, a huge structure that towers above the skyline and dwarfs everything else around it. It was begun in 1220 and you can quickly appreciate why it took over 250 years to complete. Entering through the Great West Door you see the vast nave stretching out in front of you and fluted pillars rising to flying buttresses reaching high above. There are more than 100 stained glass windows and the huge east window is almost the size of a tennis court. Guided tours leave at regular intervals. Nearby the TREASURER'S HOUSE (NT), a 17th-/18th-century townhouse on the site of the former residence of the Treasurers of York Minster, has a fine collection of furniture and an exhibition showing the development of the house from Roman times. (*Open April-October, tel 0904-624247.*)

The JORVIK VIKING CENTRE, Coppergate, is set below ground amidst the most complete Viking dig in England. Electric cars take you on a Disneyland ride backwards through history to a re-created Viking village--complete with sounds and smells of Viking Jorvik. Then they move you forward to the dig itself and a display of the artifacts that have been recovered. Because there is often a long line it is best to be there first thing in the morning for opening at 9 am. (*Open all year, tel 0904-643211.*)

Enjoy another trip back in time at York's outstanding CASTLE MUSEUM. One section of the museum is a reconstructed Victorian cobbled street, with houses, shops, jail, and a hansom cab in recognition of inventor Joseph Hansom who was born in Mickelgate. (*Open all year, tel 0904-653611.*) Opposite the museum you can climb to the ramparts of CLIFFORD'S TOWER, a stubby, 13th-century keep set high on a mound. From its ramparts you have a panoramic view of York. (*Tel 0904-646940.*)

Located beyond York's walls, just a short walk from York's magnificent Victorian railway station, is the NATIONAL RAILWAY MUSEUM, Leeman Road, crammed with famous steam locomotives including the world's fastest (125 mph), Mallard, and a wealth of railway items. (*Open all year, tel 0904-621261.*)

Depart York on the A64 Scarborough road for the fast drive to CASTLE HOWARD which is well signposted to your left just 4 miles from MALTON. Designed by Sir John Vanbrugh for the 3rd Earl of Carlisle, a member of the Howard family, Castle Howard was built between 1699 and 1726--one glimpse of this majestic building and you understand why it took 27 years to complete. Its immense facade reflects in a broad lake and it is surrounded by a vast parkland and approached down a long, tree-lined avenue. It isn't really a castle at all but one of England's grandest homes, as impressive inside as out, full of fine furniture and paintings. This grand setting is better known to many visitors as "Brideshead" from the television dramatization of Evelyn Waugh's *Brideshead Revisited*. It is still owned by the Howard family. (*Open March-October, tel 065384-333.*)

From nearby Malton take the A169 through PICKERING and across the vast expanse of the North Yorkshire Moors to ROBIN HOOD'S BAY, the most picturesque of villages situated beneath a cliff top, a maze of huddled houses, clinging to the precipitous cliff. Park in the large car park above the village and follow the long, steep street down to the shoreline, peeping into little alleyways and following narrow byways until you emerge at the slipway. Pieces of Robin Hood's Bay have been washed away, and in an attempt to minimize further damage to this little fishing village, much of the cliff has been reinforced by a large sea wall.

The ruins of Whitby Abbey face the cold North Sea and the old seaside town of WHITBY, built on either side of the River Esk. It's a lovely sight: majestic ruins high on a bleak, windy headland, rows of cottages climbing up the hillsides, and, gazing over the scene, a statue of the town's most famous mariner, Captain Cook. Cook circled the world twice, explored the coasts of Australia and New Zealand, and charted Newfoundland and the North American Pacific coast before being killed by natives in Hawaii. His home on Grape Lane is a small museum. Near Cook's statue is a whalebone arch commemorating this photogenic old town's importance as a whaling port. The whaling ships are a thing of the distant past: now just a few fishing boats bob in this large, sheltered harbor. Explore the area of the town that lies below the abbey, for this is the quaintest, most historic portion of Whitby. During the summer the town is filled with holidaymakers.

Leave Whitby on the A169, Pickering road, and follow signs to the right for the NORTH YORK RAILWAY, a road that winds you to GROSMONT, the terminus of a glorious, 18-mile steam railway that runs to and from Pickering. The railway opened in 1863 with horse-drawn carriages--steam engines came 11 years later. The line was closed by British Rail in 1965 and reopened by train enthusiasts. The railway shed is full of steam locomotives of all colors and you can see engines being prepared for their daily shift and watch restoration from the viewing gallery. (*Tel 0751-72508, fax 0751-76970.*)

From nearby EGTON a narrow road leads you up from a lush valley and onto miles of gently rolling moorland, with a mass of purple heather stretching into the distance, a dramatically empty, isolated spot, then drops you into another green valley where stone walls separate a patchwork of fields around the tiny village of ROSEDALE ABBEY. Go straight across the crossroads, up the steep bank, and across another stretch of vast moorland, keep to your right at the fork in the road and you arrive in the most picturesque village on the North York Moors, HUTTON-LE-HOLE. A tumbling stream cuts through the village and children play on close-cropped grassy banks between the sturdy stone houses. At the heart of the village lies RYEDALE FOLK MUSEUM where paths lead from a museum of domestic bygones through a collection of ancient Yorkshire buildings (from simple cottages to an elaborate cruck-framed house) rescued from demise and restored on this site. (*Open March-October, tel 07515-367.*)

Farther on from Hutton-le-Hole you join the A170 which brings you to HELMSLEY, a pretty market town beneath the southern rim of the moors. Around the market square (stalls set up on Fridays) are interesting shops and the lovely Black Swan Hotel. At the edge of town is a ruined castle enclosed by Norman earthworks.

About 4 miles beyond Helmsley (take the B1257 signed Stokesley) lie the ruins of RIEVAULX ABBEY (pronounced ree-voh), the delicate and beautiful ruins of Yorkshire's first Cistercian abbey, standing quietly beside a picturesque group of thatched cottages. The abbey fell into debt and declined until it was dissolved by Henry VIII. Today it is a graceful, ghostly ruin, often shrouded in mist. Follow the narrow lane beside the cottages, turn right over the little humpbacked bridge, proceed through SCRAWTON, and turn right on the A170 (Thirsk road) for a short distance to a left-hand turn which drops you down the Hambleton Hills escarpment into KILBURN, a village known for its fine, modern wood carving. Quality furniture found all over the world can easily be traced back here to the workshop of Robert Thompson. He died in 1955, but craftsmen he trained still use his carved signature, a small church mouse, to identify their work. It is fun to tour the workshops and watch skilled craftsmen quietly hand-carving beautiful oak furniture.

Leave the village to the right and at gaps in the hedgerow look to your right to see a large white horse carved into the distant hillside. Shortly after BAGBY turn right on the A19 and follow main roads across the flat, fertile Vale of York to RIPON where, from the obelisk in the market square, the hornblower sounds a horn at nine every evening. This once marked the start of the night watch for thieves and warned people to put out their fires.

From the center of Ripon follow well-marked signs for FOUNTAINS ABBEY (NT). Cistercian monks arrived in this sheltered valley in 1132, at about the same time they came to Rievaulx, but, unlike Rievaulx, this abbey prospered, so that by the end of the 13th century it had acquired vast estates and the abbey was home to over 500 monks. However, its prosperity did not save it from the axe of Henry VIII who sold the monastery--leaving the abbey to fall into majestic ruin. Considering that for hundreds of years it was used as a quarry for precut stone, the complex is remarkably intact. Wander over the closely cropped grass to the soaring walls of the church. Examine the few remaining floor tiles, gaze at the flying buttresses soaring high above, wander through the cloisters, and wonder at the glory that was Fountains Abbey so many years ago. Walking paths abound: a particularly pretty path is leads you across grassy meadows to the adjacent National Trust property of STUDLEY ROYAL, an 18th-century deer park and water garden. (*Open all year, tel 0765-86333.*)

Turn west (B6265) through PATELEY BRIDGE and climb higher and higher onto bleak moorlands through GREENHOW and down the fellside through HEBDEN and into GRASSINGTON, a neat village of narrow streets and cobbled squares full of shops and cafes. It's this itinerary's introduction to the Dales National Park and very crowded in summer, so you may want to park at the National Park Information Centre (useful for maps and information) and walk into town.

To experience some magnificent scenery take a breathtaking circular drive from Grassington and back again through Littondale, over the fells to Malham Cove, and back to the B6160 on the outskirts of town. Leave Grassington on the B6265, cross the River Wharfe, and turn right onto the B6160 which leads you up Wharfedale towards Kettlewell. Just after passing the huge crags that hang above KILNSEY, turn left up a narrow lane for Arncliffe. The road meanders deep into Littondale, a narrow, steep-sided, very pretty dale. At the cluster of cottages that make up ARNCLIFFE turn left for Malham and follow the narrow road as it zigzags you up the side of the dale. As the road reaches the top there is a spectacular view back into Littondale. The high, bleak moorland suddenly ends and to your left lie immense curving cliffs that drop 240 feet into a green valley. This is MALHAM COVE, one of Yorkshire's most celebrated natural features. Huddled in the valley below lies the village of MALHAM. Country lanes direct you through KIRBY MALHAM, AIRTON, WINTERBURN, HETTON, and THRESHFIELD to rejoin the B6160 which takes you back into Wharfedale.

Retrace your steps and head north to KETTLEWELL, a pretty village at the foot of Great Whernside.   In the 8th century this was an Anglican settlement, then after the Norman Conquest formed part of the estates of the powerful Percy family.   A small road leads you to the right over Great Whernside and into quiet Coverdale through WOODALE, HORSEHOUSE, and CARLTON, little villages that shelter in this pretty valley with the moors looming above.   Horses are a feature of MIDDLEHAM for there are many famous racing stables in this attractive town of gray-stone houses beneath the ruins of Middleham Castle.

Cross the River Ure and follow the A6108 into LEYBURN then turn left on the A648 and right on country lanes through REDMIRE to the crumbling ruins of BOLTON CASTLE which stands grim and square, dwarfing the adjacent village, overlooking distant Wensleydale.   You can tour several restored rooms.   The castle's most famous visitor was Mary, Queen of Scots who was held prisoner here for six months in 1568.

Minor roads take you up Wharfedale through CARPERBY (detour into AYSGARTH if you would like to walk to AYSGARTH FALLS, a series of spectacular waterfalls as the River Ure cascades down a rocky gorge) and WOODHALL to the picturesque Dales village of ASKRIGG.   Cross the river to BAINBRIDGE and take the A684 into HAWES, a bustling village whose narrow streets abound with interesting shops, good pubs, and cafes.   After exploring, leave town in the direction of Muker.   As the road climbs from the valley go right, following signs for Muker via Buttertubs.   This is one of the highest mountain passes in England (1,682 ft), rising steeply from Wensleydale, crossing dramatic high moorlands, and depositing you in narrower, wilder Swaledale.   The road gets its name "Buttertubs" from the deep, menacing, limestone pits some distance from the road near the summit.

At the T-junction follow the road to the right and cross the little bridge into

MUKER, the most charming of Swaledale's little villages--just the place to stop for a refreshing cuppa.

As you travel down Swaledale there's a feeling of remoteness: sturdy, gray-stone barns dot the stone-walled fields that checker the valley floor and rise to the green fells. GUNNERSIDE, Norse for Gunner's pasture, where a Viking chieftain herded his cattle long ago, is now an appealing village.

Through LOW ROW, FEETHAM, and HEALAUGH the enchantment of being in a narrow, secluded valley continues till at REETH the landscape opens up and the feeling of being in a wild and lonely place is gone. On through pretty countryside you continue to Richmond.

RICHMOND sits at the foot of Swaledale, a network of cobbled alleys and streets stretching from its cobbled square. At its center sits an ancient church with shops set into its walls. Overhanging the River Swale, Richmond Castle was built by Norman lords within 20 years of the Norman Conquest. Over the years only a few Scottish raiders tested the defenses of this guardian of North Yorkshire. Sweeping views across dales down to the Vale of York can be enjoyed from the top of its 11th-century ruins.

The nearby A1 will quickly guide you north into Scotland or return you south towards York.

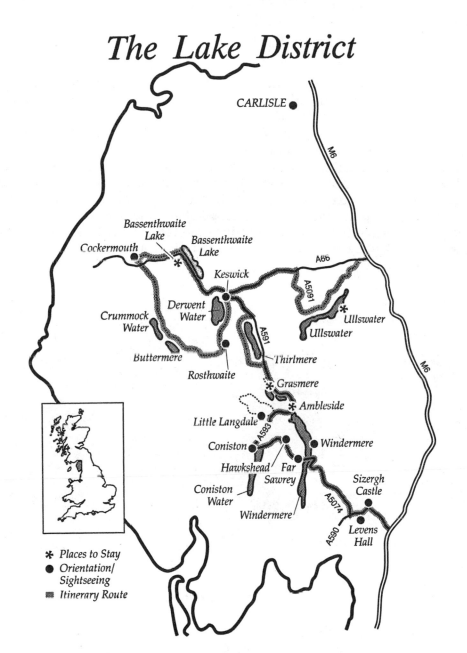

The Lake District

CARLISLE ●

M6

Bassenthwaite Lake
Cockermouth ●
Bassenthwaite Lake
✳
Keswick
A66
A5091
Crummock Water
Derwent Water
Ullswater ✳
Ullswater
Buttermere
A591
Rosthwaite
Thirlmere
Grasmere ✳
M6
Ambleside ✳
Little Langdale
A593
Coniston ●
Windermere ●
Hawkshead Far Sawrey
Sizergh Castle
Coniston Water
Windermere
A5074
A590
Levens Hall

✳ *Places to Stay*
● *Orientation/ Sightseeing*
▦ *Itinerary Route*

71

The Lake District

For generations the beauty of the Lake District has inspired poets, authors, and artists. It is a land of tranquil lakes of all shapes and sizes, quiet wooded valleys, and awesome bleak mountains, a land where much of the natural beauty is protected by the National Trust who work hard to keep this a working community of sheep farmers and keep man in harmony with nature. One of the most determined preservers of the Lake District was Beatrix Potter who used much of her royalties from her famous children's books to purchase vast tracts of land and donate them to the nation. It is a region to be explored not only during the summer when the roads are more heavily travelled and the towns crowded, but also in the early spring when the famous daffodils brighten the landscape and well into the autumn when the leaves turn to gold and dark storm clouds shadow the lakes.

The Lake District

From junction 36 on the M6 motorway take the A590 in the direction of Barrow and a few minutes' drive brings you into the grounds of SIZERGH CASTLE (NT), not a mighty fortress but a lovely, mostly Tudor house, the home of the Strickland family for over 700 years. The house is fully furnished--just as though the family has gone out for the day and you are a visitor to their home. There is an excellent teashop in the old cellar and a portion of the grounds presents an impressive rock garden. (*Open March-October, closed Fridays and Saturdays, tel 0593-60070.*)

Return to the A590 and in just a minute you are at another fine Tudor manor house, LEVENS HALL. The property is most famous for its topiary gardens which have remarkably remained unchanged since 1690, when they were landscaped by a Frenchman, Guillaume Beaumont. (*Open Easter-September, tel 05395-60321.*)

Join the A5074 Windermere road and on the outskirts of the town follow signs to the ferry which takes you across the broad expanse of Windermere for the short drive to the tiny villages of NEAR SAWREY and FAR SAWREY, discovered by Beatrix Potter on childhood holidays. She was so charmed by the villages that out of the royalties from *Peter Rabbit* she bought HILL TOP FARM (NT) in Near Sawrey. It was here in a vine-covered, stone cottage set among trees and a garden of flowers that she dreamed up childhood playmates such as Jemima Puddleduck, Mrs Tiggy Winkle, the Flopsy Bunnies, Cousin Ribby, and Benjamin Bunny. Because of its popularity the house is open on a very limited basis but the National Trust shop by the roadside is open more often and you can walk through the garden to the front door. (*Open March-October, closed Thursdays and Fridays, tel 05394-36269.*)

In nearby HAWKSHEAD, a pretty village with a pedestrian center, there is a delightful BEATRIX POTTER GALLERY (NT) containing an exhibition of her original drawings and illustrations of her children's books, together with a display of her life as author, farmer, and preserver of her beloved Lake District. (*Tel 05394-33883.*)

A short drive brings you to CONISTON, a delightful village of gray-stone buildings at the head of Coniston Water. John Ruskin, the eloquent 19th-century scholar, lived on the east side of the lake at BRANTWOOD. His home contains many mementos and pictures. (*Open mid-March-mid-November, tel 05394-41396.*) A small RUSKIN MUSEUM with drawings and manuscripts is in the village. (*Open Easter-October.*)

Travel a short distance along the A595 Ambleside road and turn left to wind along a country lane up into a quiet, less touristy part of the Lake District. Stop for refreshment in LITTLE LANGDALE at the Three Shires, a delightful, walkers' pub which also offers accommodation. Leaving the village, you enter a wild, bleak, and beautiful area. The lane brings you to Blea Tarn and just as you think you are in the absolute midst of nowhere and contemplate turning around, you come to a cattle grid and a fork in the road--take the right-hand fork signposted Great Langdale and follow the narrow road through wild and lonely countryside, down a steep pass, and through a lush valley into GREAT LANGDALE, another off-the-beaten-path village popular with walkers. Leaving the village, the road winds you up onto the moor and drops you back onto the A595 where a left-hand turn quickly brings you into Ambleside.

AMBLESIDE is a bustling, busy town with lots of shops selling walking equipment and outdoor wear and gray Victorian row houses huddling along its streets at the head of Lake Windermere. Leave town in the direction of Keswick (A591), watching for a right-hand turn to RYDAL MOUNT, the home of William Wordsworth, the poet, from 1813 to his death in 1850. The house is furnished and contains many family portraits and possessions. A keen gardner, Wordsworth laid out the 4 1/2 acres of informal gardens. (*Open March-November, closed Tuesdays, tel 05394-33002.*)

Wordsworth fans will also want to stop at DOVE COTTAGE where Wordsworth lived from 1799 to 1808 and the adjacent WORDSWORTH MUSEUM in nearby GRASMERE which the poet described as "the loveliest spot that man hath ever found." It certainly is a pretty village full of delightful shops and galleries. (*Open March-December, tel 05394-36544.*)

Dove Cottage, Grasmere

Regaining the A591, it is a delightful drive into Keswick through in turn wild, rugged, and pastoral scenery. Take small roads to the west of THIRLMERE as the views from the west of the lake are much better than from the A591.

The lively market town of KESWICK, cozily placed at the northern end of DERWENT WATER, is full of bakeries, sweet shops (selling fudge and Kendal mint cake), pubs, restaurants, and outdoor equipment suppliers. There are plenty of car parks near the town center, though on a busy summer afternoon you may have to drive around for a while before you secure a spot. The Moot (meeting) Hall at the center of the square is now the National Park Information Centre--full of maps, books, and good advice.

Returning to your car, head towards Derwent Water, taking the B5298 to Borrowdale for a spectacular drive between Keswick and Cockermouth, a journey not to be undertaken in bad weather. Follow Derwent Water to GRANGE where inviting woodlands beckon you to tarry awhile and walk, but desist because the most spectacular walking country lies ahead. Passing through the village of ROSTHWAITE, the narrow road begins to climb, curving you upwards alongside a tumbling stream to the high, treeless fells before suddenly tipping you over the crest of the mountain and snaking you down into the valley to BUTTERMERE and CRUMMOCK WATER whose placid surfaces mirror the jagged peaks that surround this wooded, green valley. The mountains here are over 500 million years old, amongst the oldest in the world. Walking paths beckon in every direction--though these are not paths to be trod without equipment and maps, for the fickle weather can turn from sun to storm in just a short while. Leaving this lovely spot, the narrow road quickly brings you into the center of bustling COCKERMOUTH where Wordsworthians have the opportunity to visit WORDSWORTH HOUSE (NT), his birthplace on Main Street. (*Open April-October, closed Thursdays, tel 0900-82405.*)

From Cockermouth follow signs for the A66 and Keswick along a country road that parallels the A66 to the head of BASSENTHWAITE LAKE. At the junction cross the busy A66 onto a quiet country side road to visit the PHEASANT INN, a superb example of the very best of traditional pubs with cozy, farmhouse-style lounges, a garden tumbling to the woods, and a wonderful, old-fashioned bar. From here the A66 quickly speeds you alongside Bassenthwaite Lake, around Keswick, and to the M6 motorway. However, if you have time for one more idyllic lake, take the A5019 through TROUTBECK to ULLSWATER where you turn left to trace the lake to AIRA FORCE (NT), a landscaped Victorian park with dramatic waterfalls, arboretum, and rock gardens (there is also a cafe). After a walk along the shores of Ullswater Wordsworth wrote his poem "Daffodils." The dramatic scenery is still very much as it was in his day. Leaving Ullswater, return to the A66 and join the M6 at junction 40, with convenient connections to all parts of Britain.

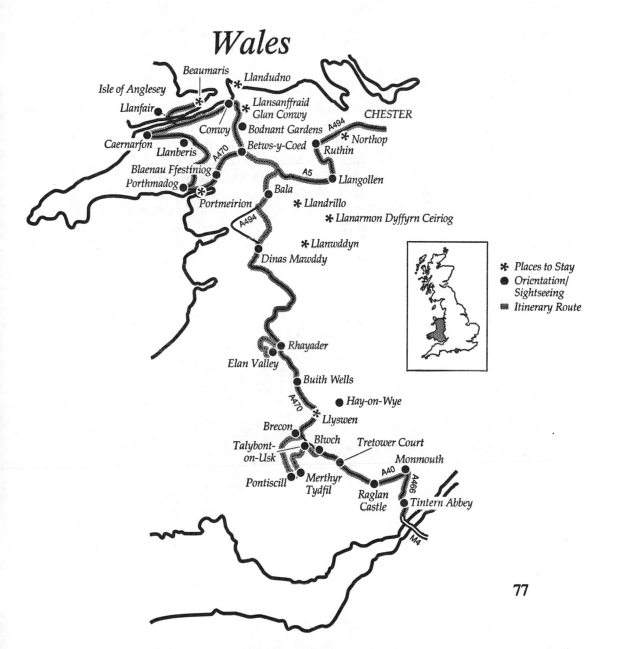

Wales

Beaumaris
Llandudno
Isle of Anglesey
Llanfair
*
Llansanffraid
Glan Conwy
*
CHESTER
Conwy
Bodnant Gardens
A494
Caernarfon
Betws-y-Coed
* Northop
Llanberis
A470
Ruthin
Blaenau Ffestiniog
A5
Porthmadog
Llangollen
*
Bala
Portmeirion
* Llandrillo
A494
* Llanarmon Dyffyrn Ceiriog

* Llanwddyn

Dinas Mawddy

Rhayader
Elan Valley
Buith Wells
A470
• Hay-on-Wye
* Llyswen
Brecon
Blwch
Talybont-
on-Usk
Tretower Court
Monmouth
Pontiscill
Merthyr
Tydfil
A40
A466
Raglan
Castle
Tintern Abbey
M4

* Places to Stay
• Orientation/
Sightseeing
▦ Itinerary Route

77

Wales

Wales has myriad towns and villages with seemingly unpronounceable names, its own language, an ancient form of Celtic, its own prince, Charles, narrow-gauge steam railways that puff contentedly through glorious scenery, and more castles per square mile than anywhere else in Europe. The Welsh have always been fiercely independent. Consequently, fortifications were built by the Welsh to defend themselves while a series of mighty fortresses was commissioned by Edward I from which the English could sally forth to subdue the fiery Welsh. Today these mighty fortresses are some of Wales's greatest treasures. Another popular attraction is the "Great Little Trains," narrow-gauge steam railway lines, with hard-working "toy" trains that once hauled slate and now steam through gorgeous countryside. And at journey's end there is bound to be a steaming cuppa to be enjoyed with bara brith, a scrumptious currant bread. As the signs say, *Croeso i Cymru*--Welcome to Wales.

Conwy Castle

Wales

Leave England on the M4 crossing the Severn toll bridge. The first indication that you are in another country is that all road signs appear in two languages, Welsh first, English second. As you leave the bridge take the first left turnoff signed A466 Monmouth and the Wye Valley. The road winds a course up the steep-sided, wooded valley to TINTERN ABBEY, a romantic ruin adored by the sentimental Victorians. Drive alongside the ruin to the car park at the rear by the tourist office. Stretch your legs with a quick walk round the ruin or, if you would like to visit the prettiest spot on the 168-mile length of Offa's Dyke, the tourist office will provide you with a detailed instruction sheet called *Offa's Dyke and the Devil's Pulpit Viewpoint*. Offa's Dyke was a great earth-work built over 1200 years ago at the direction of King Offa to divide England and Wales. (*Open April-October, tel 02918-251.*)

Follow the river as it winds into Monmouth and turn left on the A40 towards ABERGAVENNY. Travelling this dual carriageway quickly brings into view the substantial ruins of RAGLAN CASTLE, in a field to your right. Because it is on the opposite side of a divided highway you need to do an about face at the first roundabout. Raglan Castle is the last of the medieval castles, dating from the more settled later Middle Ages when its builders could afford to indulge in decorative touches. It was begun in 1431 and its Great Tower was rendered the ruin you see today by Oliver Cromwell's demolition engineers. A huge fireplace and the windows are all that remain of the grand hall but with imagination and the aid of a map you can picture what a splendid place this must have been. You can climb the battlements and picnic in the grassy grounds. (*Open April-October.*)

Stay on the ring road around Abergavenny and 2 miles after passing through CRICKHOWELL, a one-time stagecoach stop for coach travellers on the way to Brecon, turn right on the A479 to TRETOWER COURT AND CASTLE. The castle, a sturdy keep, was usurped as a habitation in the 14th century by nearby Tretower Court, a grand mansion that was the home of the Vaughan family for three centuries. As you walk through the home's empty medieval hall and along its stone passageways you can imagine how splendid a home it was. Leaving

Tretower, continue down the lane, beside the house, and turn right on the A40. (*Open all year, tel 0874-730279.*)

If the weather is fine you can enjoy an almost circular driving tour through the BRECON BEACONS by turning left towards LLANGYNIDR, and, after crossing the river, taking a right turn to CWM CRONON and TALYBONT ON USK where you turn left and follow a beautiful wooded valley alongside lakes and over the hills to PONTISCILL. On a fine day it is a spectacular drive along a narrow paved road, but this is not a trip to be appreciated when the clouds hang low over the mountains and visibility is not good. From Pontiscill the road weaves down to the outskirts of MERTHYR TYDFIL where you turn right on the A470 along another lovely valley and climb the stark, bare escarpment over the pass to BRECON.

If you do not deviate through the Brecon Beacons remain on the A40 where views of the Usk Valley and the mountains present themselves as the road climbs to the village of BLWCH. Bypass the market town of Brecon and take the A470 (Buith Wells) to LLYSWEN where you can enjoy refreshment or an overnight stay at either the Griffin Inn or Llangoed Hall. (From Llyswen an 18-mile round trip detour will afford you the chance to explore the many bookstores and antique shops of HAY-ON-WYE.)

It's a lovely drive to BUITH WELLS as the road follows the River Wye through soft, pretty countryside. Crossing the river, head to RHAYADER where an opportunity to enjoy a beautiful (in fair weather) drive through wild, rugged moorlands rising from vast reservoirs is afforded by turning left in the village for the ELAN VALLEY. Your first stop lies beneath the looming dam at the information center where a small display outlines the importance and history of clean drinking water and gives details on the vast reservoirs that provide 76 million gallons of drinking water a day. Returning to the road, follow it as it traces the reservoir through fern-covered mountains. A right-hand turn returns you to the center of Rhayader and the A470.

From Rhayader the A470 takes you quickly north. After the junction with the A458 be on the lookout for a small sign that directs you into the pretty roadside village of DINAS MAWDDY and along a narrow lane that climbs and climbs above the green fields into stark mountains, crests the pass, and winds down and around the lake to the outskirts of BALA where you make a right-hand turn immediately left on the A4212 (Trawsfyndd road) for a short distance to the B4501 which quickly brings you to CERRIGYDRUDION. There you turn left on the A5 to BETWS-Y-COED, set in a narrow, densely wooded valley at the confluence of three rivers. Crowds of visitors come to admire this town that was popularized by the Victorian painter David Cox.

From Betws-y-Coed take the A470, following the eastern bank of the River Conwy north as it winds its way to the sea. After passing through the village of TAL-Y-CAFN, look for BODNANT GARDENS (NT) on your right. Garden lovers will enjoy almost a hundred acres of camellias, rhododendrons, magnolias, and laburnum which provide incredible displays of spring color. Above are terraces, lawns, and formal rose and flower beds; below, in a wooded valley, a stream runs through the secluded, wild garden. (*Open mid-March-October, tel 0492-650460.*)

The swell of Conwy Bay is flanked by high cliffs and the town of CONWY is unforgettable for its picturesque castle set on a promontory at the confluence of two rivers and for the town's wall--over 3/4 mile in length with 22 towers and 3 original gateways. CONWY CASTLE was begun in the 13th century for Edward I and suffered the scars of the turbulent years of the Middle Ages and the Civil War. The defensive complex includes an exhibit on Edward I and his castles in Wales. On the top floor of the Chapel Tower is a scale model of how the castle and the town might have appeared in 1312. (*Open April-October, tel 0492-592398.*)

Leaving the castle, cross the road to the quay to visit a tiny home which claims to be the smallest house in Britain, then turn onto the High Street and visit the oldest house in Wales, ABERCONY HOUSE (NT). (*Open April-October.*)

Leaving Conwy, follow the A55 as it hugs the coast in the direction of Caernarfon. Rather than going directly to Caernarfon, follow signs for BANGOR (A5122) and call in at PENRHYN CASTLE (NT), a fabulous sham castle built as a grand home by a local slate magnate in the 19th century. This impressive house of intricate masonry and woodwork is filled with stupendous furniture. (*Open April-October, tel 0248-353084.*)

Cross over the Menai Straight to the ISLE OF ANGLESEY on the Menai suspension bridge, the first of its kind, built by that famous engineer, Thomas Telford, then follow the road that hugs the coast to BEAUMARIS with its closely huddled houses painted in pastel shades strung along the road. BEAUMARIS CASTLE, the last of the castles built by Edward I in his attempt to control Wales, is a squat, moated fortress with grassy grounds inside thick walls facing a harbor full of sailboats. (*Open all year, tel 0248-810361.*)

Return to the Menai bridge and, if you are inclined to have your picture taken by the sign of the town with the longest name in the world, follow directions to LLANFAIR, the abbreviation (that fits on signposts) for LLANFAIRPWLL-GWYNGYLLGOGERYCHWYNDROBWYLLLANTYSILIOGOGOGOCH which means "St Mary's Church by the white aspens over the whirlpool and St Tysilio's Church by the red cave." The drab little town has little to recommend it but commercial opportunists have cleverly situated a large shopping complex directly next to the station.

The A5 (Bangor road) quickly returns you to the mainland via the Britannia road bridge where you pick up signs for CAERNARFON. Edward I laid the foundations of CAERNARFON CASTLE in 1283 after his armies had defeated the princes of North Wales. Many revolts against English rule took place in this imposing fortress and during the Civil War it was one of Cromwell's strongholds. The first English Prince of Wales was born here in 1284. The investitures of the Duke of Windsor in 1911 and of Prince Charles in 1969 as Prince of Wales both took place in this majestic setting. This is the most massive and best preserved of the fortifications in this itinerary. It takes several hours to clamber up the towers, peep through arrow slits on the massive walls, and visit the exhibitions on the Princes of Wales, Castles of Edward I, and the Museum of the Royal Welch Fusiliers. (*Open April-October, tel 0286-77617.*)

Caernarfon Castle

Leave the coast at Caernarfon with the beauty of Snowdonia ahead of you, following the A4086 Llanberis road. The SNOWDONIA NATIONAL PARK is a region of wild mountains which, while they cannot be compared in size to the Alps or the Rockies (Snowdon rises to 3,560 ft), are nevertheless dramatically beautiful with ravines and sheer cliffs whose sides plummet into glacier-cut valleys sparkling with wood-fringed lakes and cascading waterfalls.

The village of LLANBERIS is the starting point for the ascent of the highest mountain in Wales, MOUNT SNOWDON. Easier than the rugged walking ascent is the two-hour round-trip journey on the SNOWDON MOUNTAIN RAILWAY, an adorable "toy" steam train that pushes its carriages up the mountainside on a rack-and-pinion railway. The little train winds you along the edges of precipices and up steep gradients to the mountain's summit. If the weather is fine (the train runs only in clear weather) and especially if it is July, August, or the weekend, arrive early to secure a pass which entitles you to return at an appointed time for your adventure. On the day we visited a 10:30 am arrival assured us of a place on the 4:30 pm train. Remember to take warm clothing with you as it is always cold on the summit. (*Open April-October, tel 0286-870223.*)

When you return from your mountain adventure make your way to the other side of the lake to ride the LLANBERIS LAKE RAILWAY. Rarely do you have to book in advance and the adorable little train which once served the slate quarries now puffs along 2 miles of track by the edge of the lake beneath the towering mountains. On fine days you have lovely views of Snowdon.

When you leave Llanberis the road climbs the pass and the scenery becomes ever more rocky and rugged: small wonder that Hillary and Hunt trained for the 1953 Everest ascent in this area. At the Pen-y-Gwryd hotel turn right on the A498 for Beddgelert. The landscape softens as you pass Lake Gwynant and, with the River Glaslyn as its guide, the road passes through a valley that is softer and more pastoral than those of Snowdonia's other lakes.

Crowding the river bank where three valleys meet is the little village of BEDDGELERT nestled in the foothills of Mount Snowdon. From Beddgelert, the road follows the tumbling River Glaslyn which settles into a lazy glide as it approaches PORTHMADOG, the terminus of the hard-working little FFESTINIOG NARROW-GAUGE RAILWAY which runs to and from nearby Ffestiniog. The train provides riders with a mobile viewpoint from which to enjoy the most spectacular scenery as it follows the coast and chugs up into rugged Snowdonia, at one point travelling almost in a circle to gain altitude, to terminate its journey at Blaenau Ffestiniog where, in summer, you can connect with a bus that takes you for a visit to the nearby slate caverns before returning you to the station for your return journey to Porthmadog. This rugged little train for many years carried slate from the mines to the port of Porthmadog. (*Open April-October, tel 0766-512340, 2 1/2 hours return journey.*)

A short drive on the A487 brings you to MINFFORDD where you turn right to the extravagant fantasy village of PORTMEIRION which looks like a little piece of Italy transported to Wales. It has a piazza, a camponile, and an eclectic mixture of cottages and buildings squeezed into a small space and surrounded by gardens full of subtropical plants and ornate pools. The village is a mass of color--the facades are terra cotta, bright pink, yellow, and cream and the gardens full of brightly colored flowers and shrubs. Portmeirion was the realization of a dream for Sir Clough Ellis who bought this wooded hillside plot above the broad sandy river estuary and built the village to show that architecture could be fun and could enhance a beautiful site not defile it. His architectural model was Portofino and, while there are many Italianate touches to this fantasy village, there are also lots of local recycled houses for Sir Clough rescued many old buildings and cottages from destruction (he termed Portmeirion "the home for fallen buildings") and had them transported here and erected on the site. Day visitors are charged an admission fee but if you really want to fully enjoy the fantasy (the setting for the BBC television series "The Prisoner"), spend the night at the hotel or in one of the rooms in the village and enjoy it after the visitors have left.

Leave the coast behind you and turn inland to BLAENAU FFESTINIOG where terraced houses huddle together beneath the massive, gray-slate mountain to form a village. Taking the A470 towards Betws-y-Coed, the road follows terrace upon terrace of somber gray slate up the mountainside to the LLECHWEDD SLATE CAVERNS. Exhibits show the importance of slate mining but the most exiting part of a visit here is to travel underground into the deep mine and follow a walking tour through the caverns. (*Open March-September, tel 0766-830306.*)

Continuing north (A470), a fifteen-minute drive takes you over the pass to DOLWYDDLAN CASTLE, a 13th-century keep built by Prince Llewyn that was captured by Edward I and subsequently restored in the 19th century.

From Betws-y-Coed take the A5 to LLANGOLLEN, a town that has become the famous scene of the colorful extravaganza, the International Musical Eisteddfod, the contest for folk dancers, singers, orchestras, and instrumentalists. Llangollen's 14th-century stone bridge spanning the salmon-rich River Dee is one of Wales's Seven Wonders.

Leave Llangollen on the A542 and travel over the scenic Horseshoe Pass past the ruins of the Cistercian abbey, Valle Crucis, to RUTHIN. Nestled in the fertile valley of Clwyd and closed in by a ring of wooded hills, Ruthin is an old, once fortified market town whose castle is now a very commercialized hotel complete with medieval banquets.

From here a fast drive on the A494 returns you to England and motorways which quickly take you to all corners of the realm. But before leaving the area visit the charming, medieval city of CHESTER. The Romans settled here in AD 79 and made Chester a key stronghold. Much of the original Roman wall survives, although many towers and gates seen today were additions from the Middle Ages. Chester is a fascinating city with a 2- mile path around the crest of its battlements-- the best way to orient yourself. It is fun to browse in The Rows, double-decker layers of shops--one layer of stores at street level and the other stacked on top.

Scotland

Degan Castle

Portree

Kyle of Lochalsh

A850

Sleat

A851

Ardvasar

Mallaig

A830

Glenfinnan

Loch Sunart

Tironan

Glencoe

Port Appin

A82

A85

Killin

Callander

A84

Stirling

Fort William

Drumnadrochit

Loch Ness

Whitebridge

Fort Augustus

A87

A82

Inverness

Nairn

A82

Cawdor Castle

A96

Rothes

Dufftown

A941

Kildrummy Castle

A97

Grantown-on-Spey

Braemar

A93

Ballater

Balmoral Castle

A33

A9

A924

Pitlochry

Aberfeldy

A9

Dunkeld

A984

Kinclaven

Perth

A93

Auchterarder

Dunblane

M90

Edinburgh

Aberdeen

Banchory

* Places to Stay
● Orientation/Sightseeing
▓ Itinerary Route

Scotland

Desolate and grand, the Scottish Highlands hold the appeal of all wild and lonely places. Here there is dramatic beauty to match your every expectation as heather-covered moorland gives way to wooded glens and bare, granite mountains tower above icy lochs. This itinerary journeys to Inverness via Pitlochry and the Whisky Trail, traces the shore of Scotland's most famous lake, Loch Ness, wends through the glens, over the sea to Skye, on to Fort William and Callander, and back to Edinburgh. At every turn there are echoes of history and romance--Nessie the legendary monster that inhabits Loch Ness, homes that sheltered Bonnie Prince Charlie and Flora Macdonald, the lands where Rob Roy Macgregor roamed, and Dunvegan Castle, the home of the Macleod chiefs for over 600 years. The roads are few and often narrow and the long distances between villages and small towns add to the feeling of isolation. Hauntingly beautiful in the sunshine, brooding in the drizzle, and depressing in the rain, the fickle Scottish weather offers no guarantee that the dramatic Highland scenery will be revealed. But what you can be assured of is a warm, friendly welcome from the hospitable Scots.

Edinburgh

EDINBURGH is Scotland's beautiful capital, the "Athens of the North." Ringed by hills, the city dominates an area of plateaux, steep cliffs, and deep canyons. Majestically perched on the edge of the city is EDINBURGH CASTLE, looming against the skyline. (*Open all year, tel 031225-9846.*) From the castle gates, running eastwards to Holyrood House, is a famous sequence of ancient streets, referred to as the Royal Mile. By wandering down Castle Hill, the Lawnmarket, the High Street, and Canongate, you will travel the length of the city and absorb visual traces of Edinburgh's turbulent past and legacy.

Just off the Lawnmarket is LADY STAIR'S HOUSE, where manuscripts and relics can be seen of Scotland's three most famous men of letters, Robert Burns, Sir Walter Scott, and Robert Louis Stevenson. (*Open all year, closed Sundays, tel 031225-2424.*)

On the High Street is the great ST GILES CATHEDRAL, whose role has been so important in the history of the Presbyterian Church. John Knox preached from its pulpit from 1561 until his death in 1572, hurling attacks at the "idolatry" of the Catholic Church. Behind St Giles Cathedral is PARLIAMENT HALL, a meeting place of the Scottish Parliament from 1639 until the Act of the Union with England in 1707. Today Scotland's most important courts hold sessions here. JOHN KNOX lived just a little farther down the High Street. His home has a fine oak room and an interesting collection of personal mementos. (*Open all year, tel 031556-9579.*)

Canongate, the last stretch of the Royal Mile to Holyrood, marks the boundaries of old Edinburgh. MORAYHOUSE, a 17th-century house, is located on this street and is associated with Charles I and Oliver Cromwell. HOLYROOD HOUSE was the historic home of the Stuarts, to which Mary, Queen of Scots came from France at the age of 18. The six years of her reign and stay at Holyrood made a tragic impact on her life. Shortly after marriage to a meek Lord Darnley, the happiness of the couple dissolved and their quarrels were bitter. Lord Darnley became jealous of Mary's secretary and constant companion, David Rizzio, and conspired to have him stabbed at Holyrood in the presence of the queen. Just a year later, Lord Darnley was himself mysteriously murdered and gossip blamed the earl of Bothwell. Mary, however, married the Earl promptly after Lord Darnley's death and rumors still question the queen's personal involvement in the murder. Conspiracies continued and Scotland's young queen fled to the safety of the English court. However, considering her a threat to the English Crown, Queen Elizabeth I welcomed her with imprisonment and had her beheaded 19 years later. Bonnie Prince Charlie was the last Stuart king to hold court at Holyrood in 1745. Today Holyrood, whose apartments are lavishly furnished with French and Flemish tapestries, is used by the British monarch as an official residence in Scotland. (*Open all year, closed when Royal Family in residence, tel 031556-1096.*)

Edinburgh has extravagantly allocated space for lovely gardens, parks and grand boulevards. PRINCES STREET is an elegant main thoroughfare lined by shops and hotels, and its entire south side is bordered by gardens.

The most popular time to visit Scotland's capital is during the EDINBURGH FESTIVAL. The city glows for the last three weeks of August: pipers dance down the streets and kilts are worn almost as a uniform. The hum of bagpipes sets the stage, and parades, flags, presentations, floodlights, and color appear everywhere. It is probably the most comprehensive international arts festival in the world.

Leaving Edinburgh, follow signs for the FIRTH OF FORTH BRIDGE and Perth. After crossing the Firth of Forth, the M90 takes you through hilly farmland to the outskirts of Perth where you take the A93 following signs for Scone Palace. Before reaching the palace you can detour off the main road to visit the city of PERTH. Known as the "Fair City," Perth straddles the banks of the Tay. A lovely city, it was the capital of Scotland until the 15th century; more specifically, until 1437 and the murder of James I. Following his death, his widow and young son James II moved the court to Edinburgh. One of Perth's most important historic buildings is ST JOHN'S KIRK, a fine medieval church that has been attended by many members of English and Scottish royalty. Also of interest are the PERTH MUSEUM AND ART GALLERY (*open all year*) and the MUSEUM OF THE BLACK WATCH, which is housed in Ballhousie Castle. (*Open Easter-October, closed Sundays, tel 0738-71781.*)

SCONE PALACE is a 19th-century mansion that stands on the site of the Abbey of Scone, the coronation palace of all Scottish kings up to James I. By tradition the kings were crowned on a stone that was taken from the abbey in 1297 and placed under the Coronation Chair in Westminster Abbey. This token of conquest did nothing to improve relations between Scotland and England. The present mansion is the home of the Earl of Mansfield and houses a collection of china and ivory statuettes. (*Open April-September, tel 0738-52300.*)

Continuing along the A93, shortly after leaving the abbey you pass through OLD SCONE. This was once a thriving village but was removed in 1805 by the Earl of Mansfield to improve the landscape and only the village cross and graveyard remain to mark the site.

Continue through GUILDSTOWN to STOBHALL, a picturesque group of buildings (not open) grouped round a courtyard. Once the home of the Drummond family, much of the structure dates back to the 15th century.

Cross the River Isla and continue alongside the enormous beech hedge that was planted in 1746 as the boundary of the Meikelour estate. At the end of the hedge turn left to the village of MEIKELOUR. The focal point of the village is the 1698 mercat cross, opposite which is an old place of punishment known as the Jougs Stone. Driving through the village you join the A984 Dunkeld road.

Continue through CAPUTH to DUNKELD. Telford spanned the Tay with a fine bridge in 1809, but this picturesque town is best known for the lovely ruins of its ancient cathedral. Founded in the 9th century, it was desecrated in 1560 and further damaged in the 17th-century Battle of Dunkeld. The choir has been restored. Stroll to DUNKELD CATHEDRAL by way of Cathedral Street where the little 17th- and 18th-century houses have been restored by the National Trust.

Leaving the town cross Telford's bridge and take the A9 for the 11-mile drive to PITLOCHRY where the Highlands meet the Lowlands of Scotland. The town owes its ornate Victorian appearance to its popularity in the 19th century as a Highland health resort. Now it is better known for its FESTIVAL THEATRE, whose season lasts from May to October and attracts some 70,000 theatergoers each year.

In the 1940s the local electricity company built a hydroelectric station and dam across the salmon-rich River Tummel on the outskirts of town. It is hard to imagine a power station being an asset to the town but this is certainly the case here. From the observation room at the dam you can see fish on the run as they climb the 1000-foot fish ladder around the dam and fight their way upstream to spawn in the upper reaches of the river. A special exhibition is devoted to their life cycle and the efforts being made to preserve them. (*Open April-October, tel 0796-3152.*)

The drive from Pitlochry to Braemar is spectacular. The A924 winds up from Pitlochry to the moorlands behind the town. Alternating lush green fields and heather-clad hills give way to heather-carpeted mountains as you approach the glorious Highland scenery of GLEN SHEE. Reaching the summit, you pass a winter ski resort before dropping down into BRAEMAR.

Here in the picturesque valley of the River Dee the clans gather for Scotland's most famous Highland games, the BRAEMAR GATHERING. A brilliant spectacle of pipe bands, traditional Scottish sports, and Highland dancing, the event is usually attended by the Queen and her family. Also in the village of Braemar is the cottage in which Robert Louis Stevenson lived the year he wrote *Treasure Island*.

Following the River Dee, a short drive brings you to CRATHIE CHURCH. Queen Victoria laid the foundation stone in 1895 and the Royal Family attend services here when in residence at BALMORAL CASTLE just across the river. When the Royal Family are not in residence you can visit the gardens at Balmoral and view the exhibition in the castle ballroom. Queen Victoria and Prince Albert bought this 15th-century castle in 1853 and rebuilt it in Scottish baronial style--it has been a royal summer home ever since. (*Grounds open May, June, and July whenever the Royal family is not in residence.*)

Continue into BALLATER, an attractive Highland town internationally famous for its Highland games held in August. These include many old Scottish sports and the arduous hill race to the summit of Craig Cailleach.

Leave Ballater on the A93 (Aberdeen road) and drive along the Dee Valley to the Cambus O'May Hotel, then in half a mile turn left on the A97 (signposted Huntly). The road climbs through heather-clad moorlands and then descends to the River Don valley and the ruins of KILDRUMMY CASTLE. (*Open April-September.*) Overlooking the romantic ruins of the castle and surrounded by acres and acres of beautiful gardens is KILDRUMMY CASTLE HOTEL, one of my favorite Scottish country house hotels.

The road from Kildrummy to DUFFTOWN via the little Highland villages of LUMSDEN, RHYNIE, and CABRACH takes you across broad expanses of moorland. This pleasant town was laid out in the form of a right-angled cross by James Duff, the 4th Earl of Fife, in 1817. Turn right at the Tolbooth tower in the center of the square and you come to the GLENFIDDICH DISTILLERY, the only distillery in the Highlands where you can see the complete process from barley to bottling.

Malt whisky is to Scotland what wine is to France. The rules for production are strict: it must be made from Highland barley dried over peat fires using water from streams that have run through peat and over granite and it must be distilled in onion-shaped copper stills and stored in oak vats.

Once a Highland fortress but now sadly in ruins, BALLATHIE CASTLE stands on the hill overlooking the distillery.

Four miles down the A941 you come to CRAIGELLACHIE village and distillery (the home of White Horse Whisky). Cross the River Spey and a short drive brings you to ROTHES where you can tour the GLEN GRANT DISTILLERY. Leaving the whisky distilleries of the Spey River Valley, take the A941 for 13 miles to ELGIN and the A96 for the 23-mile drive to the coast and the holiday resort of NAIRN. Boats bob in the harbor and nearby one of the old fisherman's cottages in Fishertown is a museum that shows the way of life of fisherfolk in the last century.

Shakespeare had CAWDOR CASTLE in mind when he set the scene of Duncan's death in *Macbeth*. (5 miles from Nairn on the B9090.) The present-day Thane of Cawdor shares his family home and gardens with the public. Portraits, tapestries, lovely furniture, and, of course, tales of romance and mystery blend to make this an interesting tour. (*Open May-September, tel 06677-615.*)

An 8-mile drive brings you to the cairn that marks the site of the battle of CULLODEN where on a rainy day in 1746 Bonnie Prince Charlie marched his tired rain-soaked Highlanders into hopeless battle with the English: 1,200 Highlanders were killed. This was the last battle fought on British soil and Charles's defeat led to the decline of the Highlands and the destruction of the clan system. After the battle the British hunted Charles for five months before he escaped to France. A museum documents this sad incident and on the surrounding moorland red flags outline the Scots battle plan while yellow flags denote the English. (*Open all year, tel 0463-790607.*)

Nearby INVERNESS is known as the "Capital of the Highlands." Straddling the River Ness, the town takes its name from the river and the Gaelic word "inver" meaning river mouth. Leave the town on the A82 (Fort William road) and after a mile you come to the Caledonian Canal which links the lochs of the Great Glen together to provide passage between the Irish Sea and the North Sea--the canal splits Scotland in two and without it boats would have to risk the dangerous passage around the northernmost stretches of Scotland.

Leave Inverness on the A82 (Fort William road) following the northern shore of Scotland's deepest (700 feet), longest (24 miles), and most famous lake, LOCH NESS. Keep an eye on the muddy gray waters for this is the legendary home of the Loch Ness Monster or Nessie, as she is affectionately known. So, keep an eye on the muddy grey waters of the lake and you may see more than the wind ruffling its surface. If she doesn't happen to surface for you, visit the LOCH NESS MONSTER EXHIBITION at DRUMNADROCHIT, which documents sightings that go back to the 7th century. Photographs of eel-like loops and black heads swimming give credence to the legends. (*Open all year.*)

Monster-spotting is a favorite pastime around Loch Ness and visitors gaze from the ramparts of URQUHART CASTLE because some of the best sightings have been made from here. The ruined castle dates from the 14th century and has a long and violent history. (*Open all year.*)

Following the shores of Loch Ness, a 19-mile drive brings you to FORT AUGUSTUS, a village that stands at the southwestern end of the loch. Park your car by the Caledonian Canal and wander along its banks to see the pleasure craft being lowered and raised through the locks. Thomas Telford, the famous engineer, spent from 1803 to 1847 building the sections of this canal that connect the North Sea and the Atlantic without having to navigate around the treacherous Cape Wrath.

A few miles to the southwest the little village of INVERGARRY is framed by spectacular mountain scenery. The village was burnt to the ground after the battle of Culloden because it had sheltered Bonnie Prince Charlie before and after the battle. Turn west in the village and follow the A87, through breathtaking Highland scenery, for 50 miles to Kyle of Lochalsh. The wild, rugged scenery changes with every bend in the road as you drive high above the lochs across empty moorlands then descend into glens to follow the shores of lochs whose crystal-clear, icy waters reflect the rugged mountain peaks.   Habitations are few and far between yet, until the Highland chiefs decided, in the 18th century, that sheep were more profitable than tenants, the hillsides held crofts, schools, and chapels.

Tracing the shore of LOCH DUICH, on the last lap of today's journey, EILEAN DONAN CASTLE appears, linked to the rocky shore by a bridge.   The castle is named for a saint who lived here in the 7th century.   It is a massive, walled keep that during subsequent centuries defended the coast against Danish and Norse invaders.   More recently it has been restored and it is fascinating to go into rooms with 14-foot thick walls and to climb to the battlements to see the loch spread out before you.   (*Open Easter-September, tel 059985-202.*)

Arriving at the busy fishing port of KYLE OF LOCHALSH, you see the sturdy ferry that transports cars back and forth the few hundred yards to KYLEAKIN on the ISLE OF SKYE.   The crossing takes about 10 minutes and reservations are not necessary.

There is an exhilarating feeling to the oft mist-shrouded shores of Skye where mystery and legends intermingle with dramatic scenery.   Islanders still make a living crofting and fishing, though tourism is becoming ever more important.   This is the home of the Scottish heroine Flora Macdonald who disguised Bonnie Prince Charlie as her maid and brought him safely to Skye after his defeat against the English at the battle of Culloden.

Set out to explore Skye's coastline where magnificent mountains rise from the rocky shore and sea lochs provide scenic sheltered harbors.   Skye has very good roads, although often quite narrow, making it easy to tour the island in a day.   If the weather is inclement and mist veils the island, content yourself with a good book by the fireside, for what appears stunningly beautiful on a fine day can appear dreary when sheathed in fog.

Follow the A850 (signposted Portree) through the scattered village of BROADFORD set along a broad, sheltered bay. Skirting the shoreline, you pass the island of SCALPAY before tracing the southern shoreline of LOCH AINORT. The surrounding humped peaks of the CULLIN HILLS are spectacular as you follow the road through SCONSER and SLIGACHAN to Portree.

PORTREE, the capital of Skye, is its most attractive town. Pastel painted houses step down to the water's edge, fishing boats bob in the harbor, and small boats arrive and depart from its pier. Climbing away from the harbor, the town's streets are lined with attractive shops. If you have not booked your ferry passage from Armadale to Mallaig you can do so at the Caledonian MacBrayne ferry office behind the bus station (*tel 2075*). The town derives its name from Port an Righ meaning King's Haven, following the visit in 1540 of James V who made a vain attempt to reconcile the feuding Macleod and Macdonald clans.

Cottages on Skye

Leaving the town, turn right onto the A855, a narrow, single-lane road with passing places that takes you north. As you approach the shores of LOCHS FADA and LEATHAN the jagged, craggy peaks of THE STORR (mountains) come into view. Standing amongst them is the Old Man of Storr, one of the most challenging pinnacles for mountain climbers.

Around the island's northernmost headland the crumbling ruins of the Macdonalds' DUNTULM CASTLE stand on a clifftop promontory overlooking the rocky shores of Duntulm Bay. A short drive brings you to the SKYE COTTAGE MUSEUM where four traditional Highland crofts have been restored and appropriately furnished to show a family home, a smithy, a weaver's house and a small museum. These little cottages with their thick stone walls topped by a thick straw thatch were the traditional island dwellings--very few good examples remain, though, as you travel around the island, if you look very carefully, you can see several traditional cottages in various states of ruin. Flora Macdonald is buried in a nearby graveyard. (*Open Easter-October, closed Sundays.*)

Returning to the main coastal route (A855), a short drive takes you through KILMUIR and down a steep hill into the scattered hamlet of UIG whose pier is used by ferries to the Outer Hebrides. It is here that Bonnie Prince Charlie and Flora Macdonald landed after fleeing the Outer Hebrides. Continue to KENSALEYRE and 1/2 mile beyond the village turn right onto the B8036. When this road meets a T junction turn right onto the A850 for the 22-mile drive to the village of DUNVEGAN.

Just to the north of the village is DUNVEGAN CASTLE, the oldest inhabited castle in Scotland and the home of the Macleod family for over 700 years. It stands amidst hills and moorlands guarding the entrance to a sheltered bay. After parking your car walk through rhododendron-filled gardens to the fortress. The castle's 15th-century part is known as the Fairy Tower after the threadbare Fairy Flag that hangs in one of the chambers. Legend has it that this yellow silk flag with crimson spots is the consecrated banner of the Knights Templar, taken as a battle prize from the Saracens. It is said to have the magical properties to produce victory in battle, the birth of sons and plentiful harvests. Other relics include items relating to Bonnie Prince Charlie. (*Open April-October, tel 047022-206.*)

When it is time to leave Skye take the narrow, winding road that follows the shoreline to ARMDALE. Part of Armdale Castle houses the CLAN DONALD CENTRE, a museum that tells the story of the Lords of the Isles and the Gaelic culture. (*Open Easter-October, tel 04714-305.*)

In Armdale you board the car ferry for MALLAIG, the seaport at the western end of the Road to the Isles. (*The ferry sails four times a day during the summer months and reservations should be made before sailing--it is suggested that you purchase your tickets from either the Caledonian MacBrayne ferry offices in Kyle of Lochalsh tel 4218 or Portree tel 2075.*) Leaving Mallaig, you cannot get lost for there is only one narrow road that leads you out of town (A830).

If the weather is fine you may want to pause at the spectacular white beaches that fringe the rocky little bays near MORAR. The narrow road twists and turns and passing places allow cars going in opposite directions to pass one another. The village of ARISAIG shelters on the shores of Loch Nan Ceal with views, and ferries, to the little islands of Rhum and Eigg.

From Arisaig your route turns eastwards following the picturesque shores of LOCH NAN UAMH, best known for its associations with Bonnie Prince Charlie and the Jacobite Rising of 1745. The clan leaders met in a house nearby and after his defeat the prince hid near here before being taken to the Outer Hebrides--a cairn marks the spot where he left Scotland.

More than 1,000 clansmen gathered at GLENFINNAN at the head of LOCH SHIEL to begin the 1745 Jacobite Rising. The place where they are said to have hoisted the Stuart standard is marked by a tall castellated tower. You climb the tower stairs to the statue of a Highlander overlooking the icy waters of the mountain-ringed loch. At the adjacent visitors' center the prince's exploits are portrayed.

Leaving the monument to Bonnie Prince Charlie's lost cause, follow the A830 for the 15-mile drive through KINLOCHEIL and CORPACH to Fort William. As you approach the town the rounded summit of Britain's highest mountain, BEN NEVIS, appears before you. If you are staying at Inverlochy Castle do not turn right on the A82 into town but turn left (signposted Inverness) for the short drive to the hotel whose entrance is on your left.

Bordering the shores of LOCH LINNHE, FORT WILLIAM is the largest town in the Western Highlands. While the town itself cannot be described as attractive it is the economic hub of the area and it is always crowded with tourists during the busy summer months.

From Fort William the A82 takes you southwest along the southern shore of Loch Linnhe, then turns you inland over the pass of GLEN COE, notorious for the massacre of the Macdonalds by the Campbells in 1692. After accepting their hospitality, the Campbells issued an order--written on the nine of diamonds playing card--to kill their hosts, the Macdonalds. The pass of Glen Coe is barren and rocky and the road south travels across this seemingly empty land. A short detour to KILLIN with its craft shops and impressive waterfalls provides an enjoyable break on a long drive.

Your goal is CALLANDER and a region of low mountains interspersed with serene lakes known as THE TROSSACHS. This is the country of Sir Walter Scott's novel *Rob Roy* and his poem *Lady of the Lake*. Robert MacGregor, "Rob Roy", existed as a romanticized 17th-century Robin Hood, who stole from the rich and gave to the poor. However, some regarded him more realistically as a thief and rustler! Scott's "lady" was Ellen Douglas, and her "lake" was LOCH KATRINE. There are a number of lovely lakes to view, such as LOCH ACHRAY and LOCH VENACHAR. (*Loch Katrine boat trips May-September, tel 041336-5333.*)

With a long drive behind you, allow time to take a boat along Loch Katrine, browsing in the shops on the main streets of Callander and--for the more energetic--visiting the ancient town of STIRLING, dominated by its imposing Renaissance castle. STIRLING CASTLE, once the home of Scottish kings, is perched high on a sheer cliff overlooking the battleground of BANNOCKBURN where the Scots turned the English back in their attempt to subdue the Highland clans. (*Open all year, tel 0786-62517.*)

Return to EDINBURGH, but don't leave Scotland without a promise to return!

> *"Farewell to the Highlands, farewell to the north,*
> *The birthplace of valour, the country of worth."*

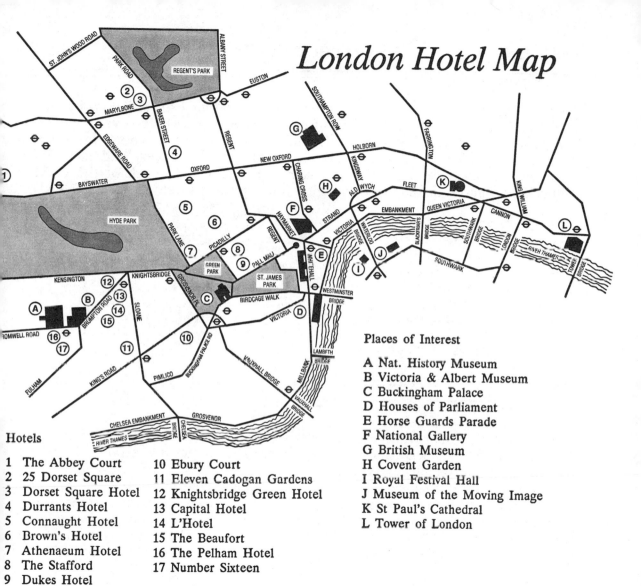

London Hotel Map

Hotels

1 The Abbey Court
2 25 Dorset Square
3 Dorset Square Hotel
4 Durrants Hotel
5 Connaught Hotel
6 Brown's Hotel
7 Athenaeum Hotel
8 The Stafford
9 Dukes Hotel
10 Ebury Court
11 Eleven Cadogan Gardens
12 Knightsbridge Green Hotel
13 Capital Hotel
14 L'Hotel
15 The Beaufort
16 The Pelham Hotel
17 Number Sixteen

Places of Interest

A Nat. History Museum
B Victoria & Albert Museum
C Buckingham Palace
D Houses of Parliament
E Horse Guards Parade
F National Gallery
G British Museum
H Covent Garden
I Royal Festival Hall
J Museum of the Moving Image
K St Paul's Cathedral
L Tower of London

From the outside The Abbey Court appears to be nothing extraordinary--just one of the many similar houses along Pembridge Gardens: one would never guess the delightful surprise awaiting within. The lobby is intimate and lovingly renovated with carefully chosen antique furniture, mirrors, wall sconces, and elaborate bouquets of flowers accentuating the fabric-covered walls. Each of the guestrooms offers maximum comfort and charm--many sport lovely, four-poster beds.

THE ABBEY COURT
Manager: Joanna Parker
Pembridge Gardens
London W2 4DU
tel (071) 221 7518   fax (071) 792 0858
22 Rooms
Single from £84, Double from £122
Credit cards: all major
Nearest underground Notting Hill Gate

The Athenaeum is an exclusive home away from home in the heart of Mayfair. It has a panelled bar specializing in Scottish whiskies, an elegant restaurant, and a classically furnished lounge serving delicious afternoon teas. The lovely bedrooms and suites are decorated in autumn, spring, or summer colors. Just a step away in a row of Edwardian townhouses with iron railings and bay windows, the Athenaeum Apartments offer an alternative to a hotel suite and have the advantage of complete privacy and impeccable kitchens. James Brown, the ebulient manager, ensures that everything is luxuriously comfortable without any air of stuffy formality.

ATHENAEUM HOTEL & APARTMENTS
Manager: James Brown
116 Piccadilly
London W1V 0BJ
tel (071) 499 3464 fax (071) 493 1860
112 rooms & 33 apartments
Single from £180, Double from £200
Credit cards: all major
Nearest underground Green Park

LONDON　　　　THE BEAUFORT　　　　Map: 15

The Beaufort is an alluring example of the small luxury hotel that has sprung up in London in more recent years.　Located in a Victorian house on a tree-lined street behind Harrods, the hotel is dedicated to making guests, particularly women, feel at home.　It is decorated in pastel colors with fresh flowers and original watercolors and all the extras such as a Walkman, a teddy bear, a VCR, access to a health club, room service, and drinks from the 24-hour bar are included in the tariff.　Breakfast is served in the room on a tray.　The sitting room with its plump sofas and chairs has a good selection of guidebooks.

THE BEAUFORT
Manager: Jane McKevitt
Beaufort Gardens
London SW3 1PP
tel (071) 584 5252 fax (071) 589 2834
29 rooms
Single from £160, Double from £175
Credit cards: all major
Nearest underground Knightsbridge

Brown's Hotel is terribly British. An old-fashioned, even Victorian, rather stuffy elegance prevails, from the panelled lounge with comfortable sofas, where guests enjoy London's best cup of tea, to the guestrooms with their traditional decor. It is no wonder that Brown's has so much character--it was founded by Byron's valet, James Brown, and was a favorite of Kipling. Brown's is a superb choice for those who want a hotel with a very British atmosphere in the heart of the theatre district.

BROWN'S HOTEL
Manager: Bruce Banister
Albermarle & Dover Streets
London W1A 4SW
tel (071) 493 6020 fax (071) 493 9381
133 rooms
Single from £155, Double from £190
Credit cards: all major
Nearest underground Piccadilly Circus

There is no sign that this Victorian townhouse in a quiet part of Chelsea is a hotel. You ring the doorbell, step into the panelled hall, sign the visitors' book, and are enveloped by the refined atmosphere of days gone by. It is rather like a discreet private club: Victorian wing chairs, guests daintily sipping afternoon tea, whispered conversations. There is no restaurant, though light meals and breakfast are available to you through room service. Bedrooms, several of which are small, are located up the panelled staircase hung with portraits. Traditional Victorian furniture is complemented by fresh decorations and modern bathrooms.

ELEVEN CADOGAN GARDENS
Manager: Mark Fresson
11 Cadogan Gardens
London SW3 2RJ
tel (071) 730 3426 fax (071) 730 5217
61 rooms
Single from £89, Double from £132
Credit cards: MC VS
Nearest underground Sloane Square

LONDON   CAPITAL HOTEL   Map: 13

The modern exterior belies the club-like atmosphere that pervades the Capital Hotel.   Bedrooms are air-conditioned and have a very masculine quality, many sporting Ralph Lauren fabrics--a few have used such dark fabrics that they appear somewhat gloomy.   The elegant, chandeliered restaurant has a much brighter air, with even a feminine flounce or two, and has one Michelin star.   Located on a quiet street just a few steps from Harrods and the Knightsbridge tube station, the Capital is the sister hotel of the adjacent, much more casual, L'Hotel.

CAPITAL HOTEL
Manager: Jonathan Orr Ewing
22 Basil Street
London SW3 1AT
tel (071) 589 5171 fax (071) 225 0011
48 Rooms
Single from £165, Double from £195
Credit cards: all major
Nearest underground Knightsbridge

Those fortunate enough to reserve a room at the Connaught will experience the charms of one of London's loveliest deluxe hotels. The Connaught deserves its reputation for unostentatious luxury, elegant charm, and quiet refinement. The restaurant too is famous--undoubtedly one of the finest in London. But the real secret of the Connaught's appeal to loyal clients is its attention to detail. Guests are warmly welcomed by name and their every preference remembered. A 15% service charge is automatically added to your bill.

CONNAUGHT HOTEL
Manager: Paolo Zago
16 Carlos Place
London W1Y 6AL
tel (071) 499 7070   fax (071) 495 3262
90 rooms
Single from £175, Double from £214
Credit cards: all major
Nearest underground Marble Arch

The Dorset Square Hotel offers excellent value for money. If you stay in one of the hotel's smallest, least expensive rooms, you find yourself enjoying the fabulous ambiance of a lovely hotel at a marvelous price. Even the most expensive small double rooms are an excellent value considering the gorgeous decor and service. Two of the first-floor balconied rooms have grand pianos. Actually, staying here is like being a guest in an exquisite English home with intimate lounges filled with flowers, lovely oil paintings, and antique furnishings.

DORSET SQUARE HOTEL
Manager: Colette Macé
39-40 Dorset Square
London NW1 6QW
tel (071) 723 7874 fax (071) 724 3328
37 Rooms
Single from £90, Double from £110
Credit cards: all major
Nearest undergrounds Marylebone & Baker Street

LONDON 25 DORSET SQUARE Map: 2

If you are travelling with family or friends, and are not on a strict budget, you will adore 25 Dorset Square, a handsome, Georgian building transformed into a marvelous, apartment-style hotel. The suites are truly scrumptious, each individually decorated, and abound with lovely antiques, country English chintzes, and stately, tall French windows, and many have fireplaces and grand pianos. And although the suites are not inexpensive, if two couples were to take one together, each could have a private bedroom and bath and live in greater grandeur for much less money than two comparable rooms would cost in one of London's fine hotels.

25 DORSET SQUARE
Manager: Paul Norman
Dorset Square
London NW1 6QN
tel (071) 262 7505 fax (071) 723 0194
12 suites
1-bedroom suite from £170
2-bedroom suite from £200
Reductions for longer stays
Credit cards: all major
Nearest undergrounds Marylebone & Baker Street

Hotels in London

Dukes is a very special little hotel--one of our favorites.   Conveniently located only steps from St James Street, Dukes is tucked into its own little gas-lit courtyard. Just off the lobby is a snug lounge and beyond is a panelled bar famous for its selection of cognacs where Salvatore, undoubtedly one of the most delightful barmen in London, holds court with a twinkle in his eye.   The restaurant is elegantly traditional.   The guestrooms are unfussy in their decor, each decorated in light colors with fine fabrics and furniture.   Dukes is a superb, luxury category hotel, but if you love cozy elegance without any air of stuffy formality, this hotel is for you.

DUKES HOTEL
Manager: Hugh Williamson-Noble
35 St James Place
London SW1A 1NY
tel (071) 491 4840 fax (071) 493 1264
62 rooms
Single from £175, Double from £205
Credit cards: all major
Nearest underground Green Park

Once a private residence, the Durrants Hotel carries the dignity and charm of an earlier age.   A wide, sweeping staircase (or an ornate, tiny lift) and beautiful, oak-panelled hallways lead to the hotel's bedrooms, all of which are comfortable, some with fine Edwardian furniture.   The old-fashioned air extends to the lounge, library, and dining room.   Durrants is close to theaterland and Mayfair.

DURRANTS HOTEL
Manager: R.C. Miller
26 George Street
London W1H 6BJ
tel (071) 935 8131 fax (071) 487 3510
104 rooms
Single from £55, Double from £95
Credit cards: all major
Nearest underground Bond Street

LONDON   EBURY COURT   Map: 10

Just a three-minute walk from Victoria station, the Ebury Court hotel has been run by the same family for more than 50 years.   It is a gem of a hotel, very friendly and very good value for money when compared to other London hotels.   Topham's restaurant (named for Diana and Roger Topham who owned and managed the hotel for so many years) offers traditional British food--breakfast is included in the room rate.   Upstairs is a rabbit warren of stairways and narrow corridors leading to an assortment of bedrooms, priced according to their size and location.   Small bedrooms are very small while the larger rooms give you space to maneuver.

EBURY COURT
Manager: Nicholas Kingsford
26 Ebury Street
London SW1W 0LU
tel (071) 730 8147
45 rooms
Single from £70, Double from £95
Credit cards: all major
Nearest underground Victoria

Close to Harrods and Hyde Park and just a few yards from the Knightsbridge tube station, the Knightsbridge Green Hotel stands out as a hotel where the staff is friendly, the location superb, and the price reasonable. It is located in a tall, narrow building where an old-fashioned lift takes you from the tiny, street-level lobby to the four floors of bedrooms. Rooms are spacious and suites have a separate sitting room. The decor is sunny, with pastel-washed walls and pretty fabrics. Bathrooms are sparkling and modern. Continental breakfast is served in the rooms. Coffee and tea are available in the small lounge during the day.

KNIGHTSBRIDGE GREEN HOTEL
Manager: Ann Thomson
159 Knightsbridge
London SW1X 7PD
tel (071) 584 6274 fax (071) 225 1635
24 rooms
Single from £84, Double from £105, Suites from £115
Credit cards: all major
Nearest underground Knightsbridge

The sister property of the adjacent Capital Hotel, this sophisticated bed and breakfast is decorated in a delightfully simple French country decor with pine furniture. There are no public rooms or room service, but the basement wine bar, Le Metro, has good-value lunches and dinners. The bedrooms vary in size; all have small, efficient bathrooms. If you book well in advance, you may be able to secure one of the three bedrooms that has a fireplace.

L'HOTEL
Manager: Karen Perkins
28 Basil Street
London SW3 1AT
tel (071) 589 6286 fax (071) 225 0011
12 rooms
Single & Double from £110, Suites £140
Credit cards: all major
Nearest underground Knightsbridge

LONDON   NUMBER SIXTEEN   Map: 17

Number Sixteen provides the atmosphere of staying in town with friends--there is even a small back garden. Guests are given front-door keys and encouraged to treat this deluxe pension as their home-away-from-home. Bedrooms are individually designed and several have a terrace onto the garden. There is no restaurant but there are a great many charming ones close by. The location is convenient--just around the corner from South Kensington tube station. Ornate plaster ceilings, bright, cheerful decor, and antique furniture further enhance the feel of a private house.

NUMBER SIXTEEN
Manager: Jane Roberts
16 Sumner Place
London SW7 3EC
tel (071) 589 5232 fax (071) 584 8615
36 rooms
Single from £60, Double from £130
Credit cards: all major
Nearest underground South Kensington

You might well pass by The Pelham thinking this is a private club, for only a classy brass plaque signifies that a hotel is within.   Inside, no expense has been spared to create a romantic, inviting atmosphere.   It has a lovely, small, panelled lounge and a beautiful, spacious restaurant with excellent cooking.   Sumptuous bouquets of flowers and gorgeous antiques set the mood of elegance without being stuffy. Accommodations range from large suites to smaller rooms with twin, queen, or king beds.   You are close to the trendy, fun boutiques and restaurants of Kensington.

THE PELHAM HOTEL
Manager: Martin Ball
15 Dromwell Place
London SW7 2LA
tel (071) 589 8288 fax (071) 584 8444
37 rooms
Single from £130, Double from £140
Credit cards: all major
Nearest underground South Kensington

The bustle of London seems far away from this quiet, refined hotel located just a short walk from Piccadilly.   Ornate plaster ceilings grace the elegant lounge and excellent dining room.   At the back of the hotel the colorful little bar has a delightful patio--the perfect place to relax on a warm day.   The most deluxe bedrooms are found in The Carriage House, a 350-year-old converted stable building.   A longtime, friendly professional staff takes pride in offering the kind of personal service that makes loyal clients return to their "home" in London.

THE STAFFORD
Manager: Dennis Beaulieu
16-18 St James Place
London SW1A 1NJ
tel (071) 493 0111 fax (071) 493 7121
74 rooms
Single from £184, Double from £200
Credit cards: all major
Nearest underground Green Park

116

Hotels in England

Rothay Manor is an exceptionally enjoyable hotel with the feel of a refined, old-fashioned British resort hotel where everything is done with kindness and without fuss.   Waitresses in ankle-length, black dresses with white mop caps graciously take your dinner order and in the afternoon an array of decorated cakes and biscuits tempts you to partake of tea.   Bedrooms are decorated in a more modern style, comfortable and spotlessly kept--those at the front have balconies opening up to the garden and are preferable to those at the rear where a busy main road can disturb a quiet night's sleep during the summer when you are likely to have your windows open at night.   A most attractive downstairs bedroom is available for those who use a wheelchair or have difficulty with stairs.   The weather report is posted in the hallway so you can be prepared for the fickle Lake District weather. The Lake District's picturesque villages and stunning scenery are easily reached by car or explored on foot.   Dove Cottage, Wordsworth's home, now a museum, is nearby.   *Directions:* From Ambleside follow signs for Coniston (A593) and you will find the hotel in the middle of the one-way system on the outskirts of town.

ROTHAY MANOR
Owners: Nigel & Stephen Nixon
Rothay Bridge
Ambleside
Cumbria LA22 0EH
tel (05394) 33605 fax (05394) 33607
18 rooms
Single from £62, Double from £98
Closed January & first week February
Credit cards: all major
Children welcome

Just off the main A6 between the delightful market town of Bakewell and the Victorian spa town of Buxton is the peaceful, sleepy village of Ashford-in-the Water.   In the center of the village, next to the ancient Sheepwash bridge, with a walled garden that borders the River Wye, Sue and Roger Taylor have their country house hotel.   Riverside has a cozy, Victorian ambiance and I always expect to see an Agatha Christie heroine like Miss Marples perched in the drawing room sipping afternoon tea.   The center of the house is the golden oak-panelled bar where a log fire burns brightly when needed.   Here, before and after dinner, drinks are served. In the adjacent dining rooms the five-course dinner is from a set menu which changes monthly.   Bedrooms in the old house vary in size while those in the "new" (albeit traditionally designed) wing are uniform in size, differently decorated, and have the advantage of immaculate modern bathrooms.   Off the beaten tourist track, Derbyshire is an area of unsurpassed beauty.   Long country walks in the Peak District National Park, visits to neighboring village pubs, and explorations of the stately Chatsworth estate, Haddon Hall, and Hardwick Hall are pursuits to be recommended.   *Directions:* Ashford-in-the-Water is 4 miles northwest of Bakewell on the Buxton road (A6).

RIVERSIDE COUNTRY HOUSE
Owners: Sue & Roger Taylor
Ashford-in-the-Water
Near Bakewell
Derbyshire DE4 1QF
tel (0629) 814275 fax (0629) 812873
15 rooms
Single from £77, Double from £99
Open all year
Credit cards: all major
Children over 10

This former pub is now an intimate little hotel with a spectacular restaurant alluringly decorated with murals depicting the seasons: winter, summer, autumn, and spring. The restaurant serves delectable French food but in winter it is closed to outside guests on Sundays and Mondays. There is a long and tempting wine list. The hotel delights in a friendly welcome from Michael Harris and his young staff. The only reminders that this was once a traditional pub are the stone-flagged bar with its windsor chairs and a portrait of Michael's father with pint in hand in the drawing room. Six bedrooms are found within the walls of the original 17th-century inn. The remainder of the bedrooms surround a flower-filled, brick courtyard in a converted brewery opposite the main building. Several of these rooms have access to the lovely walled gardens. Most of the parking is across a very busy main road by the pavilion which is used for weddings and conferences. The heart of nearby Aylesbury with its Tudor lanes and courtyards is very picturesque. If you are staying for some time you can explore Oxford, Henley, and other Thames-side towns. London is about an hour away. *Directions:* The hotel is in an urban location, in Aston Clinton, on the A41, the main London to Aylesbury road.

THE BELL INN
Owners: Patsy & Michael Harris
Aston Clinton
near Aylesbury
Buckinghamshire HP22 5HP
tel (0296) 630252   fax (0296) 631250
21 rooms
Single from £92, Double from £133
Open all year
Credit cards: all major
Children welcome

There can be no better fate for a rundown country estate than to fall into the hands of Historic House Hotels who have meticulously restored Hartwell House which opened its doors as a luxurious country-house hotel in 1989.   The Great Hall with its ornate fireplace and decorative ceiling sets the scene for the grandeur of the place, yet this is no stuffy hotel--there is a comfortable air of informality.   To the left is the oak-panelled bar which leads to the morning room and the library.   The dining room is composed of several adjoining rooms which overlook the garden. The second floor bedrooms, named after the members of the exiled King of France Louis XVIII's court who occupied them, are the largest and several have four-posters.   Cozier, and less expensive, are the attic bedrooms, some of which open out onto a sheltered roof terrace where rabbits were reared and vegetables grown by the French emigres.   More bedrooms are found in the stable building adjacent to the conference center and large indoor swimming pool.   The surrounding parkland with its ruined church, pavilion, and lake is perfect for long country walks. Oxford is just 20 miles away and Heathrow airport is less than an hour's drive.   A hotel brochure outlines three picturesque drives through nearby quaint villages. *Directions:* Hartwell House is 2 miles from Aylesbury on the A418 - Oxford road.

HARTWELL HOUSE
Manager: Jonathan Thompson
Aylesbury
Buckinghamshire HP17 8NL
tel (0296) 747444 fax (0296) 747450
48 rooms
Single from £90, Double from £135
  (Breakfast not included)
Open all year
Credit cards: all major
Children over 8

The Cavendish Hotel sits at the edge of the Chatsworth estate which surrounds one of England's loveliest stately houses, the home of the Duke and Duchess of Devonshire. Eric Marsh, the owner, has restored and expanded what was originally an 18th-century fishing inn into a fine hotel. The Garden Room (perfect for lunch and informal dinners) frames a panoramic view of the River Derwent meandering through green fields across the estate; comfy sofas and chairs in the adjacent lounge invite you to linger and enjoy. The bar is a cozy gathering spot for drinks before dinner in the highly commended dining room (you can request a table in a corner of the kitchen if you are anxious to peek at what happens behind the scenes). Most of the bedrooms in the main house have antique furniture. An adjoining wing of bedrooms has been built to match the original building and called the Mitford Rooms after their designer, the Duchess of Devonshire, and her Mitford family. These rooms are larger with more contemporary decor and modern bathrooms. A pathway leads you on a beautiful walk through the Chatsworth estate to Chatsworth House. Explorations farther afield reveal unspoilt villages set in beautiful rolling countryside of stone-walled fields, green valleys, and spectacular dales. *Directions:* Exit the M1 motorway at junction 29 and follow signs for Chatsworth through Chesterfield to Baslow.

CAVENDISH HOTEL
Owner: Eric Marsh
Baslow
Derbyshire DE4 1SP
tel (0246) 582311 fax (0246) 582312
24 rooms
Single from £74, Double from £99
Open all year
Credit cards: all major
Children welcome

Fischer's at Baslow Hall is a dream place for a relaxed getaway, with delightful cooking, especially friendly service, and the delights of the Peak District National Park on your doorstep. This superb house with its lead-paned windows set in stone frames, dark oak panelling, and wide plank wooden floors has the feeling of a Tudor manor, yet it was built only in 1907 as a home for the Reverend Jeremiah Stockdale and continued to be a home until 1988 when Susan and Max Fischer purchased it to house their successful restaurant Fischer's, relocated from nearby Bakewell, and also provide the most tasteful of accommodation. The house is furnished and decorated with imagination and flair, with a delightful use of soft yet quite vivid colors to create a feeling of warmth. Max is a dedicated chef, offering traditional English dishes as well as more elaborate fare on his mouthwatering menus. The surrounding countryside offers plenty to keep you busy for a week or longer--Chatsworth House, Haddon Hall, and (farther away) Hardwick Hall; mellow stone villages (Castleton has remarkable caves); the spa town of Buxton and glorious Peak District scenery. *Directions:* Exit the M1 motorway at junction 29 and follow signs for Chatsworth through Chesterfield to Baslow where you follow the A623, Manchester road. Baslow Hall is on the right as you leave the village.

FISCHER'S AT BASLOW HALL
Owners: Susan & Max Fischer
Calver Road
Baslow
Derbyshire DE4 1RR
tel (0246) 583259
6 rooms
Single from £70, Double from £95
Open all year
Credit cards: all major
Children over 10

From the moment you enter through the rustic porchway into the long, low, whitewashed Pheasant Inn, you are captivated by its charms: a front parlor all decked in chintz with an old-fashioned, open fire; a dimly lit, Dickensian-looking bar with tobacco-stained walls and ceiling, oak settles, and clusters of tables and chairs; a long, low-beamed dining room, its tables covered with crisp damask cloths; dramatic fresh and dried flower arrangements; a blazing fire in the hearth beneath a copper hood in the sitting room, a large, airy room, once the old farm kitchen. Bedrooms are simply yet invitingly decorated, each neat as a new pin with equally attractive modern bathrooms.   One has a half-tester bed with floral bed-ruffle and drapes--look carefully and you can see silhouettes of Albert and Queen Victoria incorporated into the design.   Behind the inn a garden with benches lining its pathways tumbles into the beechwoods which belong (as does the inn) to Lord Inglewood's estate.   The Pheasant Inn sits on a quiet country lane just out of sight of Bassenthwaite Lake.   This is a quiet part of the Lake District with beautiful views round every corner.   Sailing, boating, fishing, bird watching, and, of course, walking are available nearby.   *Directions:* The Pheasant Inn is signposted on the A66, at the head of Bassenthwaite Lake, between Keswick and Cockermouth.

PHEASANT INN
Managers: Mary & Barry Wilson
Bassenthwaite Lake
near Cockermouth
Cumbria CA15 9YE
tel (07687) 76234 fax (07687) 76002
20 rooms
From £45 per person B & B
Open all year
Credit cards: none
Children welcome

The lovely city of Bath has many treasures--fine Roman baths, the Assembly and Pump Rooms, the world's largest costume museum, fine 18th-century architecture, and a delightful shopping area. Conveniently located in a residential district on the city's outskirts is the Priory Hotel. Converted from a large private home, the hotel is close to the road in front but has two acres of lovely gardens and a swimming pool at the rear. The hotel has been decorated throughout in a traditional style to give the feeling of a country house hotel--yet you are only a 20-minute walk from the center of Bath. The restaurant is comprised of three separate rooms all facing the garden as does the spacious, French-windowed drawing room. The Priory has 21 individually decorated bedrooms, many with flowery wallpaper and coordinated drapes and bedspreads. Garden views command a premium. Among Bath's many attractions are the abbey, the Roman museum and baths, the shopping arcades, and the botanical garden. *Directions:* The Priory is located on Weston Road, on the west side of Bath, 300 yards west of one of Bath's largest parks, Victoria Park.

THE PRIORY HOTEL
Manager: Thomas Conboy
Weston Road
Bath
Avon BA1 2XT
tel (0225) 331922 fax (0225) 448276
21 rooms
Single from £100, Double from £158
Open all year
Credit cards: all major
Children welcome

If you want a hotel with room service, a restaurant, and someone to carry your bag, then The Queensberry Hotel is not for you, but if you want a small, very friendly hotel in the heart of Georgian Bath, on a quiet side street, then this is the place to stay. The ladies who run the front desk are very helpful and friendly, have lots of information on Bath, and will make dinner reservations for you at local restaurants. The drawing room is a comfortable spot to relax and read the papers. Hot and cold snacks can be served in the bar, or, in sunny weather, in the adjacent garden. Stairs go up and down, hither and yon, for the hotel is converted from three adjacent townhouses and all the staircases have been retained and interconnected one with another. What were at one time spacious principal bedrooms with their tall and often decorative plaster ceilings command the highest tariff. Attic and basement bedrooms are the least expensive--attic rooms are snug while basement rooms are large with high ceilings and large windows looking out on a narrow courtyard and up at the sidewalk. All are simply yet very tastefully appointed, with artistically draped fabrics as bedheads. A continental breakfast is served in your bedroom. *Directions:* Ask for the hotel's very specific directions on how to find The Queensberry to be sent to you when you make your reservation.

THE QUEENSBERRY HOTEL
Manager: David Brooks
Russel Street
Bath
Avon BA1 2QF
tel (0225) 447928 fax (0225) 446065
24 rooms
Single or Double from £84
Closed for two weeks over Christmas
Credit cards: all major
Children welcome

Two hundred years ago, when the gentry came to Bath to "take the waters," the Royal Crescent was the most prestigious address. Two townhouses in the center of this famous cobbled crescent have been painstakingly restored and incorporated into an elegant hotel complex with the Dower House and the Pavillion buildings reached by way of the garden. Furnished with beautiful antiques, period furniture, and valuable works of art, the hotel recreates the atmosphere of Georgian Bath which was the social center of England for many years. The elegant, high-ceilinged drawing room sets the very sedate, formal atmosphere of the hotel. An additional drawing room and the restaurant are found in the Dower House. On warm summer evenings you can eat in the garden, choosing your meal from a short menu of classic summer dishes. The sweeping central staircase or the book-lined "library" lift give access to the elegant bedrooms and sumptuous suites in the main house--many of these high-ceilinged rooms have ornate plasterwork ceilings. Equally grand suites and rooms are found across the garden. To one side of the garden is a small plunge pool where you can swim against various-strength currents. *Directions:* The crescent-shaped Royal Crescent is prominently marked on any detailed map of Bath.

THE ROYAL CRESCENT HOTEL
Manager: Simon Coombe
16 Royal Crescent
Bath
Avon BA1 2LS
tel (0225) 319090   fax (0225) 339401
44 rooms and suites
Single from £110, Double from £140
Open all year
Credit cards: all major
Children welcome

As a result of the Battle of Hastings in 1066, England's history took an unexpected course and the town of Battle earned recognition on its map.   On a hillside outside of town, the troops of King Harold and William of Normandy fought over the rightful succession to the throne.   To celebrate his victory, William, henceforth named "the Conqueror," had Battle abbey built on the site of the battlefield. Three miles from this historic site is Netherfield Place, an attractive, Georgian-style, 1920s country house personally run by Helen and Michael Collier.   They have created a very relaxed country house hotel where everything is done with a friendly smile.   A comfortable bar adjoins the lounge where you can enjoy afternoon tea or a pre-dinner drink.   The panelled dining room is popular with the locals at weekends--the food is surprisingly good value for money, incorporating many of the fruits, vegetables, and herbs grown in the walled acre and a half vegetable garden.   Bedrooms vary in size, with what were the principal bedrooms of the house being the largest and most comfortable.   Around Battle there are Bodiam Castle, Rye, Winchelsea, and gardens at Great Dixter and Sissinghurst. Farther afield lies Canterbury. *Directions:* Battle is 6 miles north of Hastings. Leave town on the A2100 (Tunbridge Wells road) and take the first left (Netherfield road) for 2 1/2 miles.   Netherfield Place is on your left.

NETHERFIELD PLACE
Owners: Helen & Michael Collier
Battle
East Sussex TN33 9PP
tel (04246) 4455 fax (04246) 4024
14 rooms
Single from £55, Double from £90
Closed for two weeks at Christmas
Credit cards: all major
Children welcome

Arriving in Blanchland gives one a sense of achievement, for it is far from the beaten path, nestling in a little valley amidst moors and forests. With little cottages, a church, and The Lord Crewe Arms set round a cobbled square, it is a fascinating village that has changed little since it was bequeathed by the Crewe family, in 1721, to a trust which administers the village. Public rooms are intriguing: the abbey kitchen is now the reception-lounge with two elegant old sofas drawn round its fire; the adjacent room has a gigantic fireplace with a "priest's hole," where General Forester hid after his band of Royalist Jacobites was defeated by Cromwell in 1715; the bar with its barrel-vaulted ceiling was once an abbey storeroom. Stairs twist up and around to the bedrooms: 17 is the largest with large windows overlooking the garden and Dorothy's Room comes complete with resident ghost, with a tiny shower room and the washbasin in the room. Across the cobbled square an additional ten bedrooms occupy The Angel, a former rival temperance hotel--September is the largest bedroom with a large attic window looking across the cobbled square. The Lord Crewe Arms is an ideal base for explorations of Hadrian's Wall. *Directions:* From Newcastle take the A69 to Hexham and turn left in the center of town for the 10-mile drive to Blanchland.

LORD CREWE ARMS
Owners: Alex Todd, Peter Lingell & Ian Press
Blanchland
near Durham
County Durham DH8 9SP
tel (0434) 675251   fax (0434) 675337
18 rooms
Single from £72, Double from £97
Open all year
Credit cards: all major
Children welcome

Woolley Grange, a gracious, 17th-century manor just outside Bradford-on-Avon, is the only listing in this guide that actively encourages families: Heather and Nigel Chapman have a very relaxed attitude towards children--they have four of their own (and a springer spaniel called Birdie). The old coach-house has been converted to a nursery (there is also a huge games room for older children) where children can spend an hour or a day. Little ones can have lunch and tea in the nursery and be tucked up in bed, or watch a video in the library while parents enjoy the most excellent of dinners in the lovely dining room--the essence of a stay at Woolley Grange is eating the most delicious food. The bedrooms are scattered throughout the rambling house and the large cottage across the courtyard. Many have old fireplaces, most have creaking old floorboards, and all have sturdy antiques and old-brass or Victorian beds topped with goose-down duvets. There is a large heated swimming pool in the grounds and bikes are available for guests' use. The area is packed with interesting things to do and places to go: historic Bath and Wells, inviting Bradford-on-Avon and Lacock, Longleat House and Safari Park, and Stourhead House and Gardens. *Directions:* Woolley Grange is 8 miles from Bath at Woolley Green, off the B3109 north of Bradford-on-Avon.

WOOLLEY GRANGE
Owners: Heather & Nigel Chapman
Woolley Green
Bradford-on-Avon
Wiltshire BA15 1TX
tel (02216) 4705 fax (02216) 4059
20 rooms
Single from £80, Double from £89
Open all year
Credit cards: all major
Children welcome

Farlan Hall is a superb place to hide away for a relaxed holiday and be thoroughly spoiled, enjoying friendly service, delightful cooking, and fine wines. It is one of only a handful of British hotels admitted to the French Relais et Chateaux group. You enter directly into the reception lounge, just the kind of comfortable room you would not mind being kept waiting in--full of sofas and chairs--a perfect spot for afternoon tea. The quality of everything, from the bountiful quantity of antique furniture to the sumptuous food, is a delight. The same quality and good taste continue to the bedrooms which vary greatly in shape and size. My favorite larger rooms are the Garden Room, just off the lounge, a grand, high-ceilinged room with an enormous four-poster bed, and the former maids' dormitory, a bright, light, flowery room whose large bathroom sports a jacuzzi tub and separate shower. While Farlan Hall is a perfect place to break your journey if you are travelling between England and Scotland, it would be a shame to spend only one night in this charming hotel. Nearby sightseeing includes Carlisle and the Roman ruins of Hadrian's Wall. Day trips can be made to the Lake District and the Scottish border towns. *Directions:* Leave the M6 motorway at junction 43 and take the A69 towards Newcastle for 12 miles to the A689. The hotel is on your left after 2 miles (not in the village of Farlan).

FARLAN HALL
Owners: The Quinion and Stevenson families
Brampton
Cumbria CA8 2NG
tel (06977) 46234 fax (06977) 46683
13 rooms
From £77 to £97 per person, dinner, B & B
Closed February
Credit cards MC VS
Children over 5 (no reduction for children)

Set in the popular, tourist-thronged Cotswold village of Broadway, The Lygon Arms has always been an inn, and records take its history back to the 14th century. It has lodged a number of important guests and a few rooms are named to honor these visitors, most impressively, both King Charles I and Oliver Cromwell. In addition to the main wing with its creaking floors, heavy beams, and charming rooms furnished with grand antique pieces, a wing with numerous contemporary rooms (admittedly with pretty fabrics) stretches behind the inn. Old adjoining properties have been taken over: the 18th-century Great Hall with its minstrels gallery is now the Lygon's restaurant; across the courtyard, behind the facade of a traditional building, is a "country club" where residents can enjoy a game of billiards, use the weight room or swim in the luxurious heated pool. Over the past six centuries the Lygon Arms has established its reputation as an excellent hotel and has perfected its services to its clients. Surrounding Broadway are the lovely Cotswold villages and towns with appealing names such as Chipping Campden, Upper and Lower Slaughter, Stow-on-the-Wold, and Upper and Lower Swell. Stratford-upon-Avon, Worcester, Bath, and Oxford are all within an hour's driving distance. *Directions:* The Lygon Arms is on the main street in Broadway, which is between Stratford-upon-Avon and Cheltenham on the B4632.

THE LYGON ARMS
Manager: Kirk Ritchie
Broadway
Worcestershire WR12 7DU
tel (0386) 852255 fax (0386) 858611
65 rooms with private bathrooms
Single from £100, Double from £145
Open all year
Credit cards: all major
Children welcome

Two miles from the hustle and bustle of Broadway are the pretty, small village of Buckland and Buckland Manor. Relax and enjoy a drink in the richly panelled lounge with its elegant furniture grouped around the fireplace where in winter a log fire blazes. In the adjacent dining room, beautiful crystal, fine china, and silverware complement the grand menu. Warm weather enables you to use the many facilities in the manicured, extensive grounds: the heated pool, tennis court, and croquet lawn. Rainy days will permit you to enjoy the tranquility of the morning room. The bedrooms are absolutely elegant, with soft beige carpets, antiques and exquisite modern bathrooms--every attention has been paid to every luxurious detail. Several bedrooms have wood-burning fireplaces and/or exquisite four-poster beds. An atmosphere of hushed gentility pervades this gracious Cotswold manor. Buckland, a peaceful village, is surrounded by other attractive Cotswold villages and is within easy reach of Stratford-upon-Avon, Warwick, and Worcester. Garden lovers will enjoy Kifsgate, Hidcote Manor, and Batsford. *Directions:* The village of Buckland is 1 1/2 miles from Broadway on the B4632.

BUCKLAND MANOR
Owners: Daphne & Roy Vaughan
Buckland
near Broadway
Worcestershire WR12 7LY
tel (0386) 852626 fax (0386) 853557
10 rooms
Single from £145, Double from £155
Open all year
Credit cards: all major
Children over 12

The clomp of hooves as horses pulled carriages down the main street of Burford has long disappeared but the inns that provided lodging and food to weary travellers remain and if you are in search of a simple, quaint hostelry you can do no better than to base yourself at The Lamb for the duration of your Cotswold stay. A tall upholstered settle sits before the fireplace on the flagstone floor of the main room, the hall table displays gleaming brass jelly-moulds, and an air of times long past pervades the place, particularly in winter when the air is heavy with the scent of woodsmoke and a flickering fire burns in the grate. Little staircases and corridors zigzag you up and down to the little bedrooms, all simply decorated in a charming cottagey style. In the dining room the four-course dinner menu, with lots of choices for each course, is priced according to what is selected for the main course. The homely little bar with its stone-flagged floor and wooden settles has an indefinable mixture of character and atmosphere. Burford's main street is bordered by numerous antique, gift, and tea shops. There are mellow stone Cotswold villages to explore and Blenheim Palace and Oxford are less than an hour's drive away. *Directions:* Burford is midway between Oxford and Cheltenham (A40). The Lamb Inn is on Sheep Street, just off the village center.

THE LAMB INN
Owners: Caroline & Richard De Wolf
Sheep Street
Burford
Oxfordshire OX8 4LR
tel (0993) 823155
15 rooms
Single from £38, Double from £70
Open all year
Credit cards: MC VS
Children welcome

Paul and Kay Henderson have achieved their goal of providing one of the finest small hotels and restaurants in England. Guests have come to expect the best and this is what they receive. Prices are high but so are the standards of luxury and the attention to detail. There are only 16 lovely bedrooms; 14 in the beautiful, Tudor-style home and 2 in a quaint, thatched cottage overlooking the croquet lawns. The largest bedrooms are on the second floor and those at the front of the house offer lovely views across the valley. The public rooms are panelled in oak with open log fires burning throughout the year. Chef Shaun Hill professionally designs the evening meal, considering the fresh produce available each day from local farmers, the hotel's own garden, and the catch from local fishermen. Paul is particularly proud of his extensive wine list, one of the finest in Britain. Chagford is a delightful country town on the edge of Dartmoor. The wild beauty of Dartmoor, with its sheltered villages and towns beneath the looming moor, has a magic all its own--country rambles and cream teas are *de rigueur* when visiting this area. *Directions:* From Chagford Square turn right (at Lloyds Bank) into Mill Street. After 150 yards fork right and go downhill to Factory Crossroad. Go straight across into Holly Street and follow the lane for 1 1/2 miles to the end.

GIDLEIGH PARK
Owners Kay & Paul Henderson, Shaun Hill
Chagford
Devon TQ13 8HH
tel (0647) 432367 fax (0647) 432574
16 rooms
Single from £170, Double from £250
 Dinner, B & B
Open all year
Credit cards: MC VS
Children welcome

Built in the 1930s as a re-creation of a medieval manor, Bailiffscourt is today a lovely country hotel. The snug, golden-stoned building is very authentic. It is constructed from medieval stone, with woodwork and windows obtained from derelict cottages, mansions, and farmhouses--all brought to Climping to re-create a medieval manor that once stood on the site. Modern plumbing is a welcome 20th-century addition. Thick stone walls, small mullioned windows, beamed ceilings, dark panelling, large open fireplaces, and pieces of medieval furniture all combine to give an "olde worlde" atmosphere. The only jarring feature is the white plastic garden furniture in the flower-filled courtyard. Stone-flagged halls, reminiscent of castle passageways, lead to the large bedrooms, eight of which have four-poster beds while nine have fireplaces. Bathrooms are large with wonderful 1930s fixtures. Room 22, a large suite, has a bathroom with side-by-side "his and hers" baths. The grounds contain tennis courts and a large swimming pool. In a parklike setting, just minutes from the sea, Bailiffscourt is an ideal base for exploring the south coast. Bailiffscourt is close to Arundel's magnificent castle, the Pavillion at Brighton, Chichester's celebrated theatre, and glorious Goodwood. *Directions:* Climping is between Littlehampton and Bognor Regis on the A259.

BAILIFFSCOURT
Climping
near Littlehampton
West Sussex BN17 5RW
tel (0903) 723511   fax (0903) 123104
20 rooms
Single from £60, Double from £90
Open all year
Credit cards: all major
Children over 8

Built in Elizabethan times as a manor house, today Kennel Holt is a tranquil country house hotel hidden from the main road by a long driveway and 6 acres of lovely landscaped grounds. Indoors antiques, beamed ceilings, and log fires (in the sitting rooms) combine to give the snug rooms an inviting atmosphere. Silver, cut glass, and candlelight provide the backdrop for the traditional English and French cuisine served. The bedrooms are named for well-known Tudor personages--Henry VIII, Raleigh, Drake, and Anne Boleyn. All are thoughtfully and comfortably furnished with antiques, TV, radio, phone, and hairdryer, with even a trouser press in some of the larger rooms. Two of the larger bedrooms contain four-poster beds. The gardens with their expanses of lawn, topiary hedges, duck pond, tree-lined paths, and vegetable plot are a delight. Cranbrook has a main street of old, white-board houses and shops and an elegant, white-board windmill. Close by are glorious Sissinghurst gardens, Tunbridge Wells, an elegant spa town, and Leeds Castle, one of the loveliest castles you will find. Chartwell, Churchill's home, and Scotney Castle with its acres of gardens are also nearby. *Directions:* Take the A21 from the M25 for 20 miles to the A262 (in the direction of Ashford). The hotel is 1 mile from the junction with the A229 at Sissinghurst.

KENNEL HOLT HOTEL
Owners: Patrick & Ruth Cliff
Goudhurst Road
Cranbrook
Kent TN17 2PT
tel (0580) 712032 fax (0580) 712931
10 rooms
Single from £62, Double from £70
Open all year
Credit cards: all major
Children over 6

At Maison Talbooth Gerald Milson and his sons Paul and David set an exceptionally high standard of service and of thought given to each guest's individual comfort and wishes. The accommodation consists of ten suites, as opposed to bedrooms, each luxuriously decorated with very silky fabrics. The bathrooms are designed to pamper--it is appropriate to quote the hotel and say that "to every bathroom there is a bedroom." Breakfast is served in your room. On a 1991 visit I was disappointed to find the hallway carpets very worn and hope that by the time you arrive they will have been replaced. If you prefer simpler, less expensive accommodation, the Milsons offer nearby Dedham Vale Hotel. In the evening a courtesy car will drive you half a mile to the celebrated Le Talbooth restaurant set in a picture-perfect, 16th-century timber-framed building nestling beside the bridge on the banks of the River Stour made famous by John Constable in his paintings. A bend in the river away from Dedham lies Flatford, a collection of cottages and a mill, and a stretch of river preserved by the National Trust to look as closely as possible as they did when Constable painted his famous pictures. *Directions:* Six miles north of Colchester exit the A12 to Dedham. Cross the river, turn right down the picturesque main street, and, on the edge of the village, first right--Maison Talbooth is on your left.

MAISON TALBOOTH
Owners: The Milson family
Stratford Road
Dedham, Colchester
Essex CO7 6HN
tel (0206) 322367 fax (0206) 322752
10 suites
Single from £82.50, Double from £106.50
Credit cards: MC VS
Children welcome

One of England's most elegant small hotels, Gravetye Manor maintains the warmth and friendliness of a private home. This is undoubtedly due to the owner Peter Herbert who is a welcoming host dedicated to making each of his guests feel very special. And he has on hand all the ingredients to ensure that those who visit have a wonderful experience: a magnificent Elizabethan manor set in acres of glorious gardens landscaped by onetime owner William Robinson who pioneered the natural look in English gardens. Inside the manor lives up to every expectation: the rooms are elegantly yet comfortably furnished with soft-toned fabrics which contrast warmly with intricately carved wood panelling. Fine antiques blend comfortably with this lovely old house. The dining room is beautiful and the food exceptional. Winnie the Pooh fans can see the house where A. A. Milne lived in Upper Hartfield and buy mementos at Pooh Corner, Christopher Robin's old sweet shop. Throughout the southeast corner of England are an abundance of glorious gardens and stately homes: Chartwell (Churchill's home), Hever Castle, Penshurst Place, Scotney Castle Gardens, and Sheffield Gardens. *Directions:* Exit the M23 at junction 10 onto the A264 signposted East Grinstead. After 2 miles, at the roundabout, take the B2028 (Haywards Heath and Brighton) and after Turners Hill watch for the hotel's sign.

GRAVETYE MANOR
Owner: Peter Herbert
Near East Grinstead
West Sussex RH19 4LJ
tel (0342) 810567 fax (0342) 810080
18 rooms
Single from £105.75, Double from £137.48
  (VAT & breakfast not included)
Open all year
Credit cards: none
Babies & children over 7

The seclusion and enchanting grounds of Combe House make it an ideal romantic retreat. A private drive originating from Gittisham village carries you to this stately, cream-tone Elizabethan mansion where John and Therese Boswell offer you a warm welcome. The grandeur of the carved panelling and the massive open log fire of the entrance hall serve to increase the welcome. The candlelit Green Dining Room enhances their son Mark's cooking. The drawing room catches the morning sun and is a choice place to linger with a pot of coffee and a well-chosen book from the adjacent library. Combe House has 15 spacious and elegant bedrooms enjoying various panoramas of the estate. There are a few bedrooms which definitely stand out. Tommy Wax, a front corner bedroom with elegant furnishings, overlooks Tommy Wax hill. The Willington and Boswell rooms are also lovely. Coombe is just a short drive from the classic Early Victorian resort of Sidmouth and Beer, a fishing village in a little bay. Nearby Axminster is famous for its carpets, Honiton for its lace. Exeter was brutally bombed in 1942 but its Norman cathedral and several of its fine old buildings survived. *Directions:* Gittisham is 13 miles south of Exeter. Take the A30 to Honiton, follow the by-pass round the town, turn left for Gittisham and follow the signs for the hotel.

COMBE HOUSE HOTEL
Owners: John & Therese Boswell
Gittisham
near Honiton
Devon EX14 0AD
tel (0404) 42756 fax (0404) 46004
15 rooms
Single from £63, Double from £97
Open all year
Credit cards: all major
Children welcome

On the hillside above the Lake District town of Grasmere, in its own secluded gardens of over 3 acres, is the Michael's Nook Country House Hotel. I was greeted on entering by a magnificent Great Dane lazily guarding a beautifully wood-panelled room decorated in antiques. My presence encouraged him to awaken and saunter out into a back room to summon his owner, Reg Gifford. With the character of an elegant country home, Michael's Nook is an ideal retreat. The ticking of a grandfather clock, antique furnishings, rich hardwood floors, oriental rugs, and flowers set the mood and atmosphere for the public rooms. Bedrooms, each varying in size and view, are named after birds and have the appropriate picture on the door. The heart of Michael's Nook is the restaurant whose deep red walls and polished tables form an elegant backdrop for a delicious five-course dinner. Reg is especially interested in wine, hence the extensive wine list. Here you have the whole Lake District to explore and at Grasmere is Dove Cottage, poet William Wordsworth's home from 1799 to 1808. Also nearby is Rydal Mount, his home from 1813. *Directions:* Take the A591 to Grasmere: do not go into the village but stay on the A591, turning right at the Swan Hotel.

MICHAEL'S NOOK
Owners: Elizabeth & Reg Gifford
Grasmere
near Ambleside
Cumbria LA22 9RP
tel (05394) 35496 fax (05394) 35765
14 rooms
From £130 to £150 per person
* Dinner, B & B*
Open all year
Credit cards: all major
Children over 12

I am so glad I found White Moss House: it is not grand or elegant but it is a gem of a cozy little hotel. It has associations with poet William Wordsworth who lived just down the road at Rydal Mount and it was lived in by his descendants until the 1930s. Now it is owned by Susan and Peter Dixon who, while giving guests their personal attention, give the same attention to detail that you find at much fancier establishments. Peter exercises his culinary talents in the five-course dinners which are freshly cooked and served in the cottage-style dining room. The small adjacent lounge guarantees conviviality amongst the guests. Each bedroom has its own character--1 is a particularly attractive twin with a ribbon-and-bow-motif running through the bedspread fabric and also has a small grassy patio. Two additional bedrooms are in nearby Brockstone Cottage. Guests have the use of a row boat for exploring and fishing on nearby Rydal Water. Lakeland scenery is glorious whether you come in spring when the famous daffodils bloom, in summer with the crowds or in autumn when the bracken and leaves turn golden brown. You can stroll to Rydal Mount and Dove Cottage, Wordsworth's famous homes. *Directions:* White Moss House is on the A591 between Ambleside and Grasmere.

WHITE MOSS HOUSE
Owners: Susan & Peter Dixon
Rydal Water
Grasmere
Cumbria LA22 9SE
tel (05394) 35295
7 rooms
From £66 to £88 per person
*   Dinner, B & B*
Open March to November
Credit cards: MC VS
Children over 8

A French name for the loveliest of English country house hotels is appropriate because this heavenly hotel is owned by a Frenchman, one of the top chefs in England, Raymond Blanc. Before you are seduced by its luxurious charms and exquisite food, it is only fair to mention that this hotel is incredibly expensive. Yet for a hotel that blends captivating surroundings with beautiful decor and exquisite food it is worth every penny. The bedrooms themselves are reason enough to come and stay--each offers the ultimate in luxury without overdoing it. Beautiful antique furniture, coordinated carpets, curtains and walls, plump beds topped by crisp, white lace pillows, and welcoming glasses of sherry. There are large bathrooms, several with gracious oval tubs, soft robes, and fluffy towels--no expense has been spared to offer the most luxurious of everything. But it is Raymond Blanc's exceptional cuisine that really makes the place--the food is outstanding (rated 2 stars by Michelin). Oxford is a 15-minute drive away, Heathrow 30 minutes, and London 45. *Directions:* Le Manoir is in the village of Great Milton, a mile from the M40 (exit 7).

LE MANOIR AUX QUAT' SAISONS
Owner: Raymond Blanc
Great Milton
near Oxford
Oxfordshire OX9 7PD
tel (08446) 8881 fax (0844) 278847
19 rooms
Double from £165
Open all year
Credit cards: all major
Children welcome

Congham Hall is a splendid country house hotel in the pretty Norfolk countryside set in 40 acres of parkland just 7 miles from the historic port of King's Lynn. Congham has paddocks and horses, a small swimming pool, a tennis court, a glorious kitchen garden full of veggies, fruits, and over 300 varieties of herbs, vast lawns, and the village cricket pitch. The lovely Georgian home is as attractive as its grounds. The house is comfortably decorated in period style. Dinner is either a five-course a la carte meal or an eight-course gourmet dinner where the first five-courses are a series of starters in the manner of the tasting menus of France. The atmosphere is quiet and serene--either Christine or Trevor Forecast is always there to offer friendly assistance. Nearby places of interest include the Queen's retreat, Sandringham, miles of quiet beaches, the historic port of King's Lynn from where George Vancouver set out to explore the northwest coast of America, and Caley Mill where sweet-scented lavender is grown. *Directions:* Take the A149 from King's Lynn towards Cromer, then at the second roundabout turn right on the Sandringham/Fakenham road. After 100 yards turn right to Grimston and Congham Hall.

CONGHAM HALL
Owners: Trevor & Christine Forecast
Grimston
near King's Lynn
Norfolk PE32 1AH
tel (0485) 600250   fax (0485) 601191
14 rooms
Single from £70, Double from £105
Open all year
Credit cards: all major
Children over 12

Near the center of England is Oakham, the once proud capital of what was England's smallest county, Rutland.   Close by is Rutland Water where you drive onto a spit of land stretching out into the middle of the lake.   At its end is the quiet village of Hambleton and a jewel of a hotel, Hambleton Hall.   The staff is caring, anxious above all else to please.   The motto over the front door echoes the relaxed, happy atmosphere: "Fay Ce Que Voudras" or "Do as you please"--I cannot imagine anyone leaving Hambleton Hall discontented.   The garden tumbles towards the vast expanse of water with rolling hills as a backdrop and behind a wall is a sheltered, heated pool.   The interior was decorated with flair by Nina Campbell and is complemented by enormous flower arrangements.   The lounge with its large inviting windows provides glorious water views.   In fine weather enjoy lunch and tea on the terrace.   Delicious smells will tempt you to the award-winning restaurant.   The bedrooms are adorable, the decorations varying from soft English pastels to the vibrant rich colors of India.   Tim Hart produces a witty booklet, "Things to do around Hambleton Hall"--shopping in Oakham and Stamford; visits to the country houses of Burghley and Belton; and trips to Cambridge and Lincoln. *Directions:* From the A1 take the A606 (Oakham road) through Empingham and Whitwell and turn left for Hambleton village and Hambleton Hall.

HAMBLETON HALL
Owners: Tim & Stefa Hart
Hambleton near Oakham
Leicestershire LE15 8TH
tel (0572) 56991 fax (0572) 724721
15 rooms
Single from £105, Double from £105
Open all year
Credit cards: all major
Children welcome

Helmsley, a collection of greystone houses grouped round a traditional market square, lies at the edge of the glorious North York Moors, an area of wild and magnificent scenery where webs of little roads cross vast stretches of heather-covered moorlands joining hamlets and villages nestling in snug green valleys. Bordering the market square a traditional old Yorkshire coaching inn has served travellers for well for over 150 years in this beautiful town. Old adjoining properties have been taken over--a Georgian house and a black and white Tudor rectory. A large new wing of rooms has been built next to the lovely back garden where old-fashioned wicker chairs are set on the lawns amongst beds of scented flowers. But The Black Swan is little changed: its higgeldy-piggledy maze of little low-beamed rooms gives it a snug feeling, its traditional furniture, lounges with old-fashioned chintzy chairs, and attentive staff all add to its charms. Eating and drinking is a great joy at The Black Swan. The chef knows how to satisfy Yorkshire tastes and appetites with traditional roasts, fillets, and chops. Fresh fish and vegetarian dishes are always on the menu. The most popular places to visit are Rievaulx Abbey, York, Castle Howard, Robin Hood's Bay, Whitby, and the folk museum at Hutton-le-Hole. *Directions:* Helmsley is on the A170 midway between Thirsk and Pickering.

THE BLACK SWAN
Manager: Steve Maslan
Helmsley
North Yorks Y06 5BJ
tel (0439) 70466 fax (0439) 70174
44 rooms
Single from £80, Double from £110
Open all year
Credit cards: all major
Children welcome

Hintlesham Hall is a serene country house hotel that you will soon come to love. The grand Georgian facade is well matched inside, with the grand salon sumptuously decorated in soft pastels highlighting its lofty ceiling. More intimate in their proportions are the pine-panelled dining room and the book-lined library lounge with its Regency red walls and soft green sofas. There is an array of bedrooms varying in size from opulent, two-story affairs, through grand, traditional four-poster rooms to small, snug bedrooms. The warm, pine-panelled bar with its comfortable sofas and chairs grouped round a large fireplace and the large book-lined library with its magnificent old billiard table are particularly inviting. Bedrooms have lovely fabrics, antiques, sparkling modern bathrooms with a profusion of toiletries, and views over miles of peaceful countryside. Just a few yards from the hotel is an 18-hole golf course. Hintlesham Hall is handily located for visiting Norwich with its beautiful cathedral and castle, Flatford Mill, the area where Constable painted several of his most famous paintings, the medieval wool towns Lavenham, Kersey, and Long Melford with their majestic churches and timber-framed buildings, and Framlingham and Orford castles. *Directions:* Just before reaching Ipswich on the A12 take the A1071 (signposted Hintlesham and Hadleigh)--Hintlesham Hall is on your right after 3 miles.

HINTLESHAM HALL
Manager: Tim Sutherland
Hintlesham near Ipswich
Suffolk IPS 3NS
tel (047387) 334   fax (047387) 463
33 rooms
Single from £85, Double from £97
Open all year
Credit cards: all major
Children welcome

Combe House Hotel is located in the Quantocks, a beautiful coastal region of Somerset, on the outskirts of the quiet village of Holford. Once a tannery and still retaining its water wheel, this soft-pink toned, rectangular cottage reflects the peace and quiet of the surrounding countryside. The resident proprietors, the Richard Bjergfelt family, see that their guests are properly taken care of. The rooms are simply but tastefully decorated with delightful prints and warm colors. The bar and lounge are also very attractive and the restaurant offers a very tasty set dinner menu. This is walking and riding country, with riding stables nearby. There are tennis courts in the grounds and a delightful, Scandinavian-style log chalet houses a heated swimming pool, sauna, and solarium. Your local explorations should include the medieval village of Dunster with its cobbled streets, yarn market, shops and famous castle, the nearby picturesque villages of Porlock and Porlock Weir, and the villages of Lynton and Lynmouth with their connecting cliff railway. *Directions:* From Bridgwater take the A39 towards Minehead. In Holford turn left at the Plough Inn and left again at the fork. Follow the small road for a 1/2 mile to the hotel.

COMBE HOUSE HOTEL
Owner: Richard Bjergfelt family
Holford
near Bridgwater
Somerset TA5 1RZ
tel (027) 874382
23 rooms
From £35 per person B & B
Closed December, January & February
Credit cards: all major
Children welcome

Essebourne Manor is very much a family affair. Michael and Frieda Yeo gave up their hotel in Scotland in 1988 when Frieda's son Simon and his great friend Mark Greenfield decided that they would like to join them in a venture. The result is a very personally run hotel that still retains the feel of a home--a welcoming home that can be yours while you stay here. Simon and Frieda ensure that guests are well taken care of while Mark makes certain that they are well fed: he terms his cooking "honest English," with the dinner menu offering a chosen fish course and plenty of choices in the other four dinner courses. Michael spends a great deal of time promoting "Pride of Britain," a consortium of privately owned hotels who believe passionately in the art of British hospitality. Bedrooms, some country cozy, others positively luxurious, are especially attractive. Six suites occupy an adjacent converted stable block where Ferndown is the honeymoon suite with a jacuzzi tub and private patio. It is a peaceful hideout for exploring many interesting places such as the cathedral towns of Salisbury and Winchester and mystical Avebury and Stonehenge. Newbury racecourse is nearby. *Directions:* From junction 13 on the M4 take the A34 south to Newbury. At the third roundabout take the A343 towards Andover. Essebourne Manor is in 8 miles.

ESSEBOURNE MANOR
Owners: Frieda & Michael Yeo,
  Simon Richardson & Mark Greenfield
Hurstbourne Tarrant near Andover
Hampshire SO11 OE12
tel (0264) 76444 fax (0264) 76473
12 rooms
Single from £84, Double from £95
Open all year
Credit cards: all major
Children over 12

At The Sign of The Angel is a black and white timbered inn at the heart of the well preserved National Trust village of Lacock. This 15th-century wool merchant's house is easy to spot as it contrasts strikingly with its neighboring stone buildings. The main dining room is a mixture of antique tables clustering around a large fire. A smaller, adjacent dining room is perfect for private parties. Dinner is always by candlelight with a traditional English roast dinner as the main course and choices being given for starters and desserts. Heavy old beams, low ceilings, and crooked walls add to the rustic elegance of the inn. The bedrooms are small and cozy with low doors, uneven creaking floors, and ancient timbers. If you have difficulty with narrow stairs and uneven floors you may prefer the ground floor room, a double-bedded room. Nestled among the bedrooms on the first floor is a comfortable, inviting residents' lounge. Two additional country-style bedrooms are found in the old farmhouse at the bottom of the garden. Be sure to leave time to visit the Fox Talbot Museum of early photographs and Lacock Abbey. Lacock is just 12 miles from Bath. *Directions:* If you are arriving from London, exit the M4 at junction 17 and take the A350 Melksham road south to Lacock.

AT THE SIGN OF THE ANGEL
Owners: The Levis family
Church Street
Lacock
near Chippenham
Wiltshire SN15 2LB
tel (024973) 230 fax (024973) 527
10 rooms
Single from £70, Double from £93
Closed last week of December
Credit cards: all major
Children over 8

Lavenham is the epitome of an "olde-worlde" English village. Many half-timbered houses line the quiet streets and continue into the market square which is dominated by a 16th-century cross and Guildhall, an impressive structure which was built in the 1520s and now contains a museum with exhibits tracing 700 years of wool trade. The Swan Inn in Lavenham is now a sophisticated hotel, but was once several houses--the town's ancient Wool Hall and humbler weavers' dwellings. Forte, the inn's owners, have tastefully joined these lovely old buildings round a courtyard garden, preserving ancient beams and whitewashed plaster and timbered walls. The delightful galleried entrance leads you to quaint, beamed lounges that beckon you to partake of a traditional afternoon tea. The hub of the hotel is its snug bar whose floor is made of bricks brought to Lavenham after being used as ships' ballast. Narrow corridors and steep staircases wind you to 47 beamed bedrooms tucked into nooks and crannies in these ancient buildings. A less expensive room, Welymot (room 5), has no view, but its ancient fireplace and woodwork positively ooze charm. A few miles hence are other delightful Suffolk villages, Kersey and Long Melford, and Constable's Flatford Mill. *Directions:* Lavenham is on the A1141 between Bury St Edmunds and Hadleigh.

THE SWAN HOTEL
Manager: Michael Grange
High Street
Lavenham
Suffolk CO10 9QA
tel (0787) 247477 fax (0787) 248286
47 rooms
Single from £75, Double from £95
Open all year
Credit cards: all major
Children welcome

Directly you walk into the oak-panelled hall, you catch the spirit of this lovely house with its enormous stone fireplace, ornate, stone mullioned windows, and plump sofas enticing you to sit and relax. The adjacent panelled dining room has the same comfortable, inviting atmosphere. The dark oak panelling, the carvings and the ornate plasterwork ceilings are embellishments added by Lewtrenchard Manor's most famous owner the Reverend Sabine Baring Gould who composed the hymns "Onward Christian Soldiers" and "Now the Day is Over." The bedrooms are all different, named after the melodies of the Reverend's tunes--Melton and Prince Rupert are four-poster rooms. Sue and James run the house themselves and guests appreciate the homelike atmosphere. You do not see many hotelkeepers making tea for guests, serving drinks in the bar, and chatting in front of the fire with guests as Sue does. You cannot beat this hotel for friendliness and hospitality. Within a short drive are Castle Drogo, a fanciful Lutyens house, Lydford Gorge, an outstanding beauty spot, Dartington Glass, wild Dartmoor, and the north and south coasts of Devon. *Directions:* From Exeter take the A30 towards Bodmin and Oakhampton. After 6 miles of single carriageway (just after the Lewdown motel) turn left at the sign marked Lewtrenchard 3/4 mile.

LEWTRENCHARD MANOR
Owners: Sue & James Murray
Lewdown
near Oakhampton
Devon EX20 4PM
tel (056683) 256 fax (056683) 332
8 rooms
Single from £70, Double from £95
Closed for three weeks in January
Credit cards: all major
Children over 8

Down a mile-long driveway, this grand and dignified Georgian mansion stands in 100 acres of parkland and fields, with a fine terrace enjoying bucolic views for summer drinking and lazing, and plump sofas in the panelled drawing room for relaxing. Built in 1750, it belonged to various lords and ladies then served variously as a boys' school, ecumenical college, and home for Vietnamese boat people before being restored to its original splendor and transformed into a country house hotel. Up the grand staircase, bedrooms come in every shape and size. Several smaller bedrooms are found in the adjacent courtyard cottages. Small executive conferences are sometimes held here but they do not intrude and help the hall keep up its high standards of service and meals. Plans are afoot for the addition of a leisure center with swimming pool, sauna, and gymnasium. Nearby is Harewood House, its magnificent interior created by Robert Adam, its gardens by Capability Brown. Visitors enjoy the multitude of fine things in York, go shopping in Harrogate, explore the Yorkshire Dales, and visit the Bronte parsonage at Haworth. *Directions:* From Wetherby take the A661 (Harrogate) for a 1/2 mile. Turn left for Linton and at the center of the village, opposite the Windmill pub, turn right for Wood Hall.

WOOD HALL
Manager: Alistair Forrest
Linton
near Wetherby
West Yorkshire L522 4JA
tel (0937) 587271 fax (0937) 584353
22 rooms
Single from £98, Double from £108
Open all year
Credit cards: all major
Children welcome

The Rising Sun, dating back to the 14th century, has a prime, waterfront location in the picturesque fishing village of Lynmouth. At one time The Rising Sun was supposedly a smugglers' haven. A whitewashed building with a heavy thatched roof houses the heart of the inn where you find the bar and dining room which oozes character from its dark wooden panelling and low-beamed ceiling. The guest-rooms are located in cottages that step up the hill from the heart of the inn following the contours of the street. Crooked hallways and slanting floors attest to these homes' age. Bedrooms are small and all similarly decorated with light wooden furniture. By far our favorite accommodation is found in the picture-perfect, thatched, rose-covered cottage where Shelley honeymooned in 1816. Perched above the hotel on a private terrace, the cottage has a lounge, kitchen, and bedroom with four-poster bed. Lynmouth is joined to its neighboring village of Lynton by a funky old cliff railway--Lynmouth nestles at the foot of the cliff and Lynton with its attractive Victorian houses sits at the top. Inland lies wild and beautiful Exmoor made famous by Blackmore in *Lorna Doone*. *Directions:* Lynmouth is on the A39 between Barnstaple and Minehead.

THE RISING SUN
Managers: Hugo & Pamela Jeune
Harbourside
Lynmouth
North Devon EX35 6EQ
tel (0598) 53223 fax (0589) 53480
16 rooms
Single from £38, Double from £76
Shelley's cottage £106
Open all year
Credit cards: all major
Children over 5

On a secluded hillside stands the small gray Elizabethan manor house that is Riber Hall.   The hall is found beyond the town of Matlock, overlooking the small hamlet of Riber.   This attractive mansion has been carefully restored from a ruin by Gill and Alex Biggin and Alex's mother.   Riber Hall opened first as a restaurant and is now also a luxury hotel.   Crackling logs blaze in the enormous, ornate, dark wood fireplace that dominates the lounge where guests gather for drinks before dinner. The candlelit dining rooms are a blend of polished wood, gleaming silver, and sparkling crystal.   On a rainy or cold evening it must be difficult to stir from the warm, intimate house for the walk across the courtyard to the converted stables which house the bedrooms.   The big attraction of the bedrooms is that all but one have beautiful, antique Jacobean and Elizabethan four-poster beds.   When I arrived, the receptionist was enthusiastically describing each of the bedrooms to a gentleman making a reservation by phone.   Nearby are the jewels of Derbyshire-- rolling green dales, lovely villages, medieval Haddon Hall, and the magnificent Chatsworth estate. *Directions:* Exit the M1 at junction 28 (Chesterfield) and take the A615 (Matlock road) to Tansley where you turn left at the Murco petrol station, up Alders Lane to Riber Hall.

RIBER HALL
Owner: Alex Biggin
Matlock
Derbyshire DE4 5JU
tel (0629) 582795 fax (0629) 580475
11 rooms
Single from £84, Double from £99
Open all year
Credit cards: all major
Children over 10

Wander across the fields to the sea or explore the lovely surrounding area and return to Chewton Glen for tea in the garden ablaze with flowers. This is a heavenly way to pass the fading afternoon hours. When the chill of the evening starts to stir, it is wonderful to know that Chewton Glen provides a comforting warmth, which in turn beckons you indoors to the beauty and privacy of your own room. Chewton Glen is an outstanding luxury hotel that is continuously improving. Now Martin Skan's dream of perfection has 60 rooms (in the main house and adjacent converted stables). With a hotel this size it is hard to keep a feeling of warmth but he has done it. There are several attractive bars and lounges decorated with bright print fabrics. Chewton Glen is famous for its fine dining room (it has a Michelin rosette) and has one of the finest wine lists in Britain. There are tennis courts, croquet, a beautiful, heated swimming pool set beneath a balustraded terrace, and a health club complex with pool, gym, tennis, and various treatments. The New Forest where wild deer and ponies roam on miles of moorland is nearby. At Romsey is Broadlands, home of the late Lord Mountbatten, a lovely Palladian house with riverside grounds. *Directions:* From the A35 follow signposts for Highcliffe (not New Milton), go through Walkford then turn left down Chewton Farm Road--the hotel is on your right.

CHEWTON GLEN
Owner: Martin Skan
New Milton
Hampshire BH25 6QS
tel (0425) 275341 fax (0425) 272310
60 rooms
Double from £190
Open all year
Credit cards: all major
Children over 7

In the oldest part of Penzance, on a narrow street overlooking the harbor, is The Abbey Hotel. With his penchant for house restoration and her love of antiques, Michael and Jean Cox purchased and restored the hotel, turning it into the gem it is today. Soft blues and pinks throughout provide a background for the old pine furniture, country antiques, and interesting old knickknacks. The ambiance is informal: on arrival you are given a key to the front door. There are no bedroom door keys. If you have any questions, just pop your head round the kitchen door and ask. The second floor contains the three choice bedrooms: room 1 is especially attractive, with its large patchwork quilt-covered bed, fireplace, comfy chairs, and huge, pine-panelled bathroom with large antique tub. Room 3 has a delightful sitting nook and a bathroom hidden behind a bookcase door. Room 4 has twin beds covered with hand-embroidered covers and inviting window seats providing views of the harbor; a shower and WC are tucked into a large closet. Penzance is a lively resort with a fascinating smuggling history. Nearby are St Michael's Mount, Mousehole, a quaint old fishing village, and Land's End (this is very commercialized so go instead to Cape Cornwall). *Directions:* On entering Penzance stay on the seafront road; just before the bridge (across the harbor) turn right and immediately left up the slipway--The Abbey Hotel is at the top of the hill.

THE ABBEY HOTEL
Owners: Jean & Michael Cox
Penzance
Cornwall TR18 4AR
tel (0736) 66906
6 rooms
Single from £60, Double from £77
Open all year
Credit cards: none
Children over 5

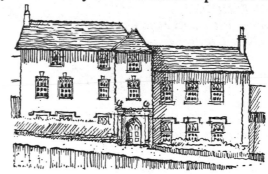

Stone House, the manor house for Rushlake Green, has belonged to the Dunn family for over 500 years. Built in 1432 with an addition in 1778, this glorious house is filled with wonderful antique furniture and old English china which is complemented by chintzes and family memorabilia. There is a croquet lawn and an antique, full-size billiard table. Bedrooms vary in size but nearly all have old beams and are furnished with care and provided with almost everything you might need from TV to hot water bottles, sewing kit, books, and tempting biscuits. Two rooms are gorgeous, four-poster suites with equally lovely bathrooms--one of the bathrooms is decorated with antique samplers. Dinner and breakfast are served in the oak-panelled dining room and continental breakfast is available in your bedroom. Nearby is the Glyndebourne Opera house, where from May to September great singers and conductors perform. Nearby, Churchill's home, Chartwell, and Rudyard Kipling's home, Bateman's, are very popular. Glorious gardens include Sissinghurst, Great Dixter, Scotney Castle, and Sheffield Park. *Directions:* From Heathfield take the B2096 towards Battle and then the fourth turning on the right to Rushlake Green. Turn left in the village (with the green on your right) and Stone House is on the far left-hand corner of the crossroads.

STONE HOUSE
Owners: Peter and Jane Dunn
Rushlake Green
near Heathfield
East Sussex TN21 9QJ
tel (0435) 830553   fax (0435) 830726
8 rooms
Single from £72, Double from £95
Open May to October
Credit cards: none
Children over 9

Rye is beautiful: once a busy port, it became marooned 2 miles inland when the sea receded. Rye was once the haunt of smugglers who smuggled wool to France and returned with brandy, lace and salt. Climb the narrow cobbled streets to one of the smugglers' favorite haunts, The Mermaid Inn. This ancient, timbered inn is a historic delight-- traces of lovely oil paintings remain on the dark wood panelling. You will find yourself spending time in the popular, inviting bar warmed by a fireplace which is large enough to stand in, and even longer hours enjoying dinner in the restaurant. Creaking staircases lead to beamed bedchambers and secret passages which add validity to the tales of pirates and smugglers. Less expensive bedrooms are bland and characterless. A bedroom to request is Dr Syn's bedchamber. Spacious, with two grand wooden beds, leaded glass windows, a beamed ceiling, and a sunken small bathroom, it also has a hidden staircase, to be found--where else?--behind the bookcase and leading down to the bar. Places to visit in the town include the Town Hall, the church, the town model, Lamb House (home of author Henry James), and the Ypres Tower and museum. Inland lies Bodiam Castle. Bird-watchers enjoy the nature reserves at Romney Marsh and Rye Harbour. *Directions:* Rye is on the A259 between Folkestone and Hastings.

THE MERMAID INN
Owner: Michael Gregory
Mermaid Street
Rye
East Sussex TN31 7EU
tel (0797) 223065 fax: (0797) 226995
28 rooms
Single from £68, Double from £105
Open all year
Credit cards: all major
Children over 8

I was actually thankful for the rainstorm which drove me inside to the shelter and warmth of The Greenway's beautiful drawing room and lounges.   (Having noticed the inviting drawing room on arrival, I found any excuse to retire to it very welcome.)   A peaceful afternoon reading before a crackling log fire happily took the place of an abandoned walk in the hillsides.   What bliss to listen to the gentle rainfall!   An equally delightful evening was spent in the conservatory dining room overlooking the lily pond and, in the far distance, the Cotswold hills: lit by dancing candles, it set the mood for an intimate, delicious dinner.   Upstairs, the luxurious, handsomely furnished bedrooms overlook the surrounding countryside.   Another block of equally luxurious bedrooms is located beside the house.   Situated on the edge of the Cotswolds and not far from the Welsh Marches, The Greenway is an ideal place from which to explore.   If you are a devoted sightseer, I might almost recommend you bypass The Greenway, as it is so hard to leave and might upset your scheduled itinerary.   The lovely Georgian spa town of Cheltenham is just a few minutes' drive away and you can quickly reach the heart of the Cotswolds with its lovely villages.   *Directions:* The Greenway is located in a somewhat suburban area 2 1/2 miles south of Cheltenham on the Cheltenham to Stroud road.

THE GREENWAY
Owner: Tony Elliott
Shurdington
near Cheltenham
Gloucestershire GL51 5UG
tel (0242) 862352   fax (0242) 862780
18 rooms
Single from £105, Double from £130
Closed Christmas to mid-January
Credit cards: all major
Children over 7

Ston Easton Park is one of the most elegant country house hotels in England. Decoration of the grand, Palladian-style rooms has been supervised by an acknowledged authority on 18th-century decoration. Sumptuous period antiques are found in all the rooms. The most impressive room is the grand salon with its high, ornate plaster ceiling, intricate carved pediments over the doorways and fireplace, carefully arranged groups of chairs and sofas around a lovely circular table--and an attentive maid hovering just out of sight. I enjoyed the less formal atmosphere of the snug library where comfortable chairs are grouped around a blazing log fire and the walls are lined with books in their mahogany bookcases. Explorations "downstairs" show the other side of life in the 18th century--the old servants' hall, kitchen, linen room, wine cellar, and billiard room--all restored and in use on a day-to-day basis. Upstairs the principal bedrooms have lovely four-poster beds with matching hangings and curtains. Outside you can stroll through the parklike grounds (created by Humphrey Repton in 1793) or play croquet on the lawn of this serene mansion. Ston Easton is a perfect touring base for forays to Bath, Bristol, Wells, Salisbury, Glastonbury, Longleat, and Stonehenge. *Directions:* Ston Easton Park is just off the A37, 6 miles northeast of Wells.

STON EASTON PARK
Owners: Peter & Christine Smedley
Ston Easton
near Bath
Avon BA3 4DF
tel (076) 121631 fax (076) 121377
21 rooms
Single from £105, Double from £140
Open all year
Credit cards: all major
Children over 12

Just 50 miles south of London, Tim and Pauline Ractliff have created a small luxury hotel of such warmth that you feel as though you are staying in an elegant private home. Little Thakeham is a fine example of a Lutyens, Tudor-style mansion, with tall brick chimneys and small diamond-paned windows. Deep, comfortable armchairs and sofas grouped round the fireplace welcome you to the large two-storied sitting room in the center of the house. To one side is the comfortable bar and to the other the gracious, oak-furnished dining room. Beautiful pieces of Art Deco glassware are displayed throughout the house. The bedrooms are particularly appealing, with views out of the little stone-mullioned windows across the garden to acres and acres of orchards. Stroll along the flagged paths through the garden before dinner or, if inclined to more energetic pursuits, take advantage of the heated outdoor swimming pool. During the cricket season you may well see Mr Ractliff and his team demonstrating their skills on their pitch--the large lawn that separates the gardens from the orchards. Guests head for Petworth House to see Turner's paintings, the Weald and Downland Museum of Rural Life, and Arundel Castle. *Directions:* Take the A283 (Pulborough road) from Storrington, turn right towards Thakeham and Merrywood Lane is to the right.

LITTLE THAKEHAM
Owners: Pauline & Tim Ractliff
Merrywood Lane
Storrington
West Sussex RH20 3HE
tel (0903) 744416 fax (0903) 745022
9 rooms
Single from £90, Double from £150
Closed over Christmas
Credit cards: all major
Children welcome

Plumber Manor has been a country home of the Prideaux Brune family since the early 17th century.   Portraits hanging in the upstairs gallery hint at the grandeur of the family's past. (There is also a portrait of Charles I which he personally presented to his mistress, a member of the family.)   Billed as a "restaurant with bedrooms," Plumber Manor is under the personal supervision of the family. Richard and Alison Prideaux Brune look after guests;   Brian Prideaux Brune, the chef, conscientiously provides a high standard of cuisine and wine. Six comfortable, spacious bedrooms are in the main house and just across the garden ten rooms surround a courtyard.   Our favorites are 14, 15, 16 and 17--spacious, two-level rooms with luxurious modern bathrooms.   Ten miles away lies Milton Abbas, a picture-perfect village of thatched cottages built in 1770 by the Earl of Dorchester who had razed the old village because it interfered with his view. Another pretty village is Cerne Abbas with thatched and Tudor cottages, 7 miles north of Dorchester (Hardy's Casterbridge). Within reach are Salisbury, Longleat, and the many attractions in and around Bath.   *Directions:* In Sturminster Newton turn left from the A352 onto the road leading to the village of Hazelbury Bryan.   Plumber Manor is 1-1/4 miles beyond on the left.

PLUMBER MANOR
Owners: The Prideaux Brune family
Hazelbury Bryan
near Sturminster Newton
Dorset DT10 2AF
tel (0258) 72507 fax (0258) 73370
16 rooms
Single from £60, Double from £85
Closed February
Credit cards: all major
Children over 12

Fronting directly onto the main street of this delightful Cotswold town, the severe stone facade of The Close gives you no idea that behind its facade lies a refreshingly different country house hotel that backs onto a restful, flower-filled garden.   The lobby with its faux marble pillars and decorative paintwork hints at the strikingly different paint treatments found throughout the hotel. A grand piano sits in a nook between the two dining rooms and a pianist treats guests to jazz and 30s tunes on most Saturday evenings.   While several rooms are decorated in a traditional flowery motif, several are refreshingly contemporary: one is Art Deco and one is Art Nouveau--you either love it or hate it.   Likewise, there is a wide range of room rates, luxurious rooms being more than twice the price of standard rooms. Rose, Tower, and Doves are exquisite, four-poster rooms. The best advice is to discuss rates and decor at the time of booking.   Tetbury is a delightful town.   Popular sights include Westonbirt Arboretum, Slimbridge Wildfowl Trust, Berkley Castle, Bath, and Cheltenham. *Directions:* Tetbury is on the A433.   The Close is on Long Street, the main street through town.   Instructions on how to get to the private car park are posted on the front of the hotel.

THE CLOSE
Owners: Peter and Richard Reeves
Long Street
Tetbury
Gloucestershire GL8 8AQ
tel (0666) 502272 fax (0666) 504401
15 rooms
Single from £55, Double from £75
Closed for two weeks in January
Credit cards: all major
Children over 10

Tucked away at the edge of the small town of Thornbury is Thornbury Castle and from the moment you see it you will be enchanted. Construction began in 1510 at the order of the Duke of Buckingham but ceased when he was beheaded in 1521 at the Tower of London. Henry VIII visited Thornbury with Anne Boleyn and Mary Tudor lived here before becoming queen. Carol and Maurice Taylor continue the upkeep of this partially restored castle, leaving other areas as a romantic ruin. Dinner in the baronial dining rooms is a leisurely affair. Soft-carpeted hallways lead to the bedrooms--this is no longer a castle of drafty stone passages. The rooms are elegantly decorated as befits their castle surroundings, several with four-poster beds; all have private bathrooms. The large octagonal tower room has a four-poster bed and its own turret staircase. Nearby Slimbridge Wildlife Trust was founded by Sir Peter Scott (son of the explorer) in 1946. Just south of Slimbridge is Berkley and Berkley Castle where Edward II was murdered in the dungeon in 1327. Also in the grounds is the Jenner museum, a tribute to Edward Jenner, discoverer of the smallpox vaccination. *Directions:* At the junction of the M4 and M5 motorways take the A38 north to Thornbury. At the bottom of the hill in the High Street fork left down Castle Street and the entrance to the castle is on your left.

THORNBURY CASTLE
Owners: Carol & Maurice Taylor
Thornbury near Bristol
Avon BS12 1HH
tel (0454) 418511   fax (0454) 416188
18 rooms
Single from £75, Double from £95
Open all year
Credit cards: all major
Children over 12

Touching the water's edge, the Sharrow Bay Hotel has one of the most glorious views in England--a panorama of Ullswater mirroring the surrounding mountains. Francis Coulson and Brian Sack bought the hotel in 1948 armed with a vision of a country house hotel and for many years Sharrow Bay has been the yardstick by which other luxury country house hotels are measured.   The warmth and welcome of Brian Sack and Francis Coulson plus the wonderful five-course dinner make a visit to Sharrow Bay Hotel a memorable one.   Bedrooms are furnished with antiques and come with absolutely everything, even when they are of very cozy proportions.   Twelve lovely bedrooms are in the main house, the remainder in cottages nearby or just down the road at Bank House where guests enjoy breakfast in the beamed refectory dining room, larger bedrooms, and stunning views of the lake from this hillside location.   Idyllic Lake District scenery is on your doorstep tempting you to go no farther than the terrace patio.   Close by are plenty of good walks, fishing, and boating. *Directions:*   Exit the M6 at junction 40 onto the A66 towards Keswick.   At the roundabout take the A592 towards Lake Ullswater. Turn left at the lake then go through Pooley Bridge where you turn right at the church, following signs for Howtown to Sharrow Bay.

SHARROW BAY HOTEL
Owners: Francis Coulson & Brian Sack
Manager: Nigel Lawrence
Ullswater near Penrith
Cumbria CA10 2LZ
tel (07684) 86301 fax (07684) 86349
30 rooms
From £118 dinner, B & B per person
Closed January and February
Credit cards: none
Children over 13

Lower Slaughter, just down the lane from its sister village, Upper Slaughter, is a quiet, tranquil collection of idyllic cottages surrounded by bucolic Cotswold countryside. At its edge lies the former home of the Witt family, "lords of the manor" hereabouts for over 200 years--a massive portrait of the Reverend Witt sitting regally on his stallion graces the landing on the main staircase. Facing lush, rolling countryside, the main house with its well proportioned, high-ceilinged rooms oozes country house charm and peacefulness--three of the five largest bedrooms have four-posters. Cleverly blended into this large home is a curving wing of rooms built to appear like other farm buildings that overlook the narrow lane. Smaller than the grander rooms of the main house, these rooms are smartly outfitted and have well equipped bathrooms. A walk leads through the fields to the old mill at Lower Slaughter. It is a perfect location for forays through the Cotswolds: nearby Lower and Upper Swell are very picturesque; Broadway and Bourton-on-the-Water are best visited early in the morning to avoid the crowds. The Cotswold Farm Park with its rare farm animals is nearby. *Directions:* From the A429 on the outskirts of Bourton-on-the-Water a small signpost indicates "The Slaughters." Follow the lane through Lower to Upper Slaughter.

LORDS OF THE MANOR HOTEL
Manager: Richard Young
Upper Slaughter
near Cheltenham
Gloucestershire GL54 2JD
tel (0451) 20243 fax (0451) 20696
29 rooms
Single from £75, Double from £97.50
Open all year
Credit cards: all major
Children welcome

Standing on the River Frome, this 16th-century building was once the priory for the adjacent church and is now a particularly lovely hotel. The entrance, through a little walled courtyard, sets a cozy ambiance. Inside, the lounge, intimate bar, dining-breakfast room and charming cellar restaurant are very pleasant, with a comfortable, homey decor. Upstairs the guestrooms are all individually furnished: some are very large and beautifully decorated while others are less elaborate and priced accordingly. The most expensive and sought-after accommodation are three deluxe suites in the Boat House which fronts onto the river. The gardens are well worth a visit--a lush lawn stretches down to the River Frome and the stone terrace is surrounded by glorious roses. Wareham is an interesting mix of architectural styles encircled by earth banks built by the Saxons to keep marauding Viking raiders out of their village. The church is Saxon and contains a memorial to Lawrence of Arabia whose home at nearby Clouds Hill is open to the public. There are many wonderful places to visit, such as Lulworth Cove, Corfe Castle, Poole Harbor, Wool, Bindon Abbey, and Durlston Head. *Directions:* Wareham is on the A351 between Poole and Swanage.

THE PRIORY
Owners: John & Stuart Turner
Church Green
Wareham
Dorset BH20 4ND
tel (0929) 552772 fax (0929) 554519
19 rooms
Single from £70, Double from £85
Open all year
Credit cards: all major
Children by arrangement

Sitting in a large informal garden surrounded by miles of open farmland, this unpretentious little hotel offers countryside peace and quiet, a relaxed place where you are cushioned from the hurly-burly of the world.   The Victorian exterior of the house contains a much older interior, evidenced by the beamed entrance hall, the old wooden latch doors, and the low-beamed ceilings.   Whether you are taking tea by a blazing log fire in the sitting room or relaxing in the sun-lounge, you feel at home.   The dining room overlooks a wisteria-covered terrace and Diana offers Old English as well as conventional fare on her short menu.   Up the winding cottage staircase the bedrooms are all different and very pleasant, each named after a hill in the nearby Malvern range.   A warm welcome is given to children and there is a large garden where they can play.   Many guests visit the Royal Worcester porcelain factory in Worcester, 15 miles away (you must make an appointment to tour the factory where you can also purchase "seconds" at bargain prices).   Nearby Hereford, Gloucester, and Worcester have fine cathedrals and the Cotswolds are an easy daytrip away.   *Directions:* Take junction 1 off the M50 and turn north on the A38 (Worcester).   After 2 miles turn left on the A4104 through Upton-on-Severn and Welland to Holdfast Cottage Hotel.

HOLDFAST COTTAGE HOTEL
Owners: Diana & Dennis Beetlestone
Welland
near Malvern
Worcestershire WR13 6NA
tel (0684) 310288
8 rooms
Single from £34, Double from £64
Open all year
Credit cards: MC VS
Children welcome

The Wykeham Arms is a very extraordinary Victorian pub: over 600 pictures decorate the walls, 1,000 tankards hang from beams, walls, and windows, and Winchester memorabilia abounds--many of the tables are old desks from nearby Winchester College. The menu, posted on the board in the bar, offers choices ranging from elaborate fare to tasty pub grub. Quieter tables can be reserved in the Bishop's Bar or the Watchmaker's Room with its pictures of an old-time watchmender. A family bible sits atop a lectern outside the breakfast room. Up narrow stairways, the pretty bedrooms are not elaborate; several have views across the chimney tops. Small refrigerators are stocked with very reasonably priced drinks. Because The Wykeham Arms is located in a pedestrian zone, all is peace and quiet (except on Friday morning when barrels of beer are rolled across the cobbles at 6.30 am). You can wander the lovely old streets, stroll through the King's Gate and across the lawns to Winchester Cathedral with its seven chapels, medieval wall paintings, and royal tombs, and walk to everything in Winchester. *Directions:* Winchester is between junctions 9 and 10 on the M3. The Wykeham Arms is located near the cathedral. Graeme will send you a map which will enable you to navigate your car through the pedestrian zone to the pub's car park.

THE WYKEHAM ARMS
Owners: Anne & Graeme Jameson
75 Kingsgate Street
Winchester
Hampshire SO23 98T
tel (0962) 853834 fax (0962) 854411
7 rooms
Single from £62.50, Double from £72.50
Open all year
Credit cards: none
Children over 14

Winsford is a lovely, tranquil Exmoor village centered on a village green on the River Exe. At the heart of the village, with its thick thatched roof curving around its upstairs windows, is the Royal Oak Inn. Legend has it that the highwayman, Tom Faggus, held up patrons of the inn and R. D. Blackmore, hearing of his exploits, used him as a character in "Lorna Doone." Upstairs the bedrooms, with low ceilings and "olde-worlde" charm, are decorated in a fresh, cottagey style. The Royal Oak Suite is an extra large room with a high, beamed ceiling, a large brass bed, a spacious bathroom, and a private staircase leading to the lounge. Across the courtyard are five annex rooms with contemporary fitted furniture (I had difficulty distinguishing my closet door from my bathroom door) and matching flowery wallpaper and drapes. Overstuffed chairs and sofas grouped round a blazing log fire set the warm country atmosphere of the lounges. The dining room offers country-style food served in generous portions. A most appealing feature is the traditional pub, its bar crowded with locals and visitors--it is a most convivial place to gather after a day's sightseeing. Exmoor was once a royal hunting domain and is a national park with a great variety of scenery--part is rolling farmland, much is vast expanses of rolling heathland, and to the north it dips to the sea. *Directions:* Winsford is 20 miles south of Minehead, just off the A396.

ROYAL OAK INN
Owners: Sheila & Charlie Steven
Winsford
Somerset TA24 7JE
tel (064) 385455 fax (064) 385388
14 rooms
Single from £55, Double from £75
Open all year
Credit cards: all major
Children welcome

Langley House hotel lies at the heart of Somerset. This handsome, two-story, peach colored house reflects a Georgian influence, yet the home dates back to the 16th century. The owners, Anne and Peter Wilson, run their small, elegant hotel with great professionalism that is enhanced by a sincere warmth of welcome. The lounge, bar, and dining room are tastefully decorated and exude an ambiance of a refined private home. Fires blazing in open hearths and well-chosen antiques add to the comfortable country-house atmosphere. The dining room is especially attractive in the evening when candles glow on beautifully set tables. The food is excellent and much of the produce comes from the hotel's walled garden. The individually decorated bedrooms are well equipped: we particularly appreciated the glasses of sherry and the bouquet of flowers. Langley House is surrounded by the Quantocks, the rolling hills of Exmoor that include the Doone valley. Dunster with its old yarn market and the pretty villages of Selworthy and Porlock are well worth a visit. *Directions:* Leave the M5 at junction 25. At the center of Wivelscombe turn left, signposted Langley Marsh: the hotel is on your right after 1/2 mile.

LANGLEY HOUSE
Owners: Anne & Peter Wilson
Langley Marsh
Wivelscombe
Somerset TA4 2UF
tel (0984) 23318 fax (0984) 24573
8 rooms
Single from £60, Double from £79
Closed February
Credit cards: all major
Children welcome

Blenheim Palace, Queen Anne's gift to the Duke of Marlborough for his defeat of Louis XIV's army in 1704, is one of England's most splendid stately homes. The Marlboroughs were also Churchills, which explains why Winston Churchill was born here in 1874--his mother was visiting relatives when she went into labor. In the adjacent town of Woodstock, The Bear Inn is owned by the Duke of Marlborough who supervises its decor and upkeep while the day-to-day operations are managed by the Forte group of hotels. As you might expect in a historic hostelry that was first licensed as an inn in 1232, there is a lot of "olde-worlde" charm, though it seems a shame that a great deal of the very old-fashioned woodwork has been coated with black gloss paint. The bar, with its heavy beams and old-fashioned Windsor chairs round a large stone fireplace, is delightful. The creaking, 16th-century staircase leads to the residents' lounge overlooking the square and the bedrooms. There are several old-fashioned, four-poster rooms. New rooms have been added over the years: some are uniform and rather plainly decorated. Blenheim Palace is a short walk and Oxford half an hour away on the bus (parking can be a problem). *Directions:* Woodstock is 8 miles from Oxford on the A34.

THE BEAR HOTEL
Manager: Chris Holden
Park Street
Woodstock
Oxfordshire OX20 1SZ
tel (0993) 811511 fax (0993) 813380
45 rooms
Single from £85, Double from £110
 (Breakfast not included)
Open all year
Credit cards: all major
Children welcome

Four 17th-century townhouses at the very heart of this delightful Cotswold town have been cleverly interwoven to create this charming hotel. This accounts for the maze of little staircases going seemingly every which way up and around to the bedrooms. Bedrooms are all different: several have high ceilings and all are decorated in soft, muted colors in a most appealing, country-house style. Nightingale is a most attractive suite overlooking the garden. The dining room, decked out in vivid blue and yellow, is enhanced by dramatic, large flower arrangements. There is a large drawing room upstairs. A central log fireplace burns a cheery blaze in the bar with its rush-matted floor and peach-washed walls. An especially cozy nook is the tiny flagstone-floored room with its country-style chairs. French windows open up to a small garden where tables, benches, and colorful hanging baskets are encircled by a high stone wall--a lovely sheltered spot to enjoy lunch in the summer. The small town of Woodstock is at its best after the crowds have left. Early mornings or summer evenings are especially good times to stroll through the parklike grounds of the adjacent Blenheim Palace. Oxford is 8 miles away and Stratford-upon-Avon 32 miles. Lovely Cotswold villages are on your doorstep. *Directions:* Market Street is off Oxford Street, which is the A34 Oxford to Stratford-upon-Avon road.

THE FEATHERS
Manager: Tom Lewis
Market Street
Woodstock
Oxfordshire OX20 15X
tel (0993) 812291 fax (0993) 813158
17 rooms
Single from £75, Double from £90
Credit cards: all major
Children welcome

York, where Romans walked, Vikings ruled, and Normans conquered, is a fascinating city, its historical center encircled by a massive stone wall. The Grange, a lovely townhouse hotel, lies just beyond the city walls and five minutes' walk from the Minster (cathedral), making it an ideal spot for exploring this wonderful city. The morning room, which leads directly off the marble lobby, has a rich, traditional feel with its Turkish carpet and Victorian portrait hung over the fireplace. The Ivy Restaurant's dramatic saffron yellow decor was chosen to enhance the gilt-framed oil paintings of St Ledger winners on loan from the York Racehorse Museum. The basement Brasserie offers simpler, lighter fare. Each of the bedrooms--some with canopied, four-poster, or half- tester beds--has different decor: several are very dramatic. I much prefer the softer, brighter, chintzier looking bedrooms to the rather somber, dark-colored rooms which appear somewhat gloomy on dark days. York takes several days to explore: attractions include the Minster, Betty's teashop, the Jorvik Viking museum, the Treasurer's House, the medieval street of The Shambles, the castle and its adjacent museum, walks along the walls, and a boatride on the River Ouse. *Directions:* The Grange is located along Bootham which is the A19, York to Thirsk road. There is ample, off-street parking to the rear of the hotel.

THE GRANGE
Manager: Andrew Harris
Clifton
York Y03 6AA
tel (0904) 644744 fax (0904) 612453
29 rooms
Single from £85, Double from £98
Open all year
Credit cards: all major
Children welcome

Middlethorpe Hall is an imposing, red-brick William and Mary country house built in 1699 for Thomas Butler, a successful cutler who wished to distance himself from his industrial success and establish himself as a country gentleman. It has been skillfully restored by Historic House Hotels and is now a very grand hotel, but without one iota of stuffiness or snobbishness. The two panelled dining rooms have large windows overlooking the grounds. After enjoying elegant, country-house fare you retire to the enormous, graceful drawing room for coffee, chocolates, and liqueurs round the fire watched over by the massive portraits of long departed gentry. Up the magnificent carved oak staircase, bedrooms enjoy high ceilings, tall windows (those at the back with views across the grounds), and Edwardian-style bathrooms. Additional, very attractively decorated bedrooms are in the stable block across the courtyard. York (a ten-minute drive away) will keep you busy for at least two days--add Castle Howard, explorations of the dales, moorlands, and the coast, and you can justify a week in this most superlative of country house hotels. *Directions:* The hotel is situated just outside the village of Bishopthorpe, next to the racecourse. Exit the A64, Leeds to Scarborough road, at the A1036, Tadcaster to York road, and follow the hotel's map.

MIDDLETHORPE HALL
Manager: Andrew Bridgeford
Bishopthorpe Road
York Y02 1QP
tel (0904) 641241 fax (0904) 620176
30 rooms
Single from £91, Double from £120
 (Breakfast not included)
Open all year
Credit cards: all major
Children over 8

Hotels in Scotland

Francis Atkins is considered to be one of the most innovative chefs in Scotland and the hospitality of Farlayer House is well known. The house dates back to the 16th century when it was built as a croft on the estate of the nearby Castle Menzies which is being restored by the clan. Following the 1745 Rebellion, the croft was extensively enlarged and eventually became the main residence of the head of the clan. Now sitting in 70 acres of parklike and wooded grounds, Farlayer House has been refurbished to provide a lovely backdrop for Francis's culinary skills. Warm golden pine on the doors, the staircase, and panelling gives an atmosphere of coziness and warmth. The upstairs drawing room is the hotel's most prominent room: rugs cover some of the old wooden floor, sofas and chairs are arranged in inviting groupings, and tall windows frame views across the parklike grounds. Bedrooms vary in size from small attic rooms tucked under the eaves to larger, more elegantly decorated rooms which were the principal bedrooms when this was a home. Atholl Palace, Cluny Gardens, Bolfraks Gardens, and vistas of delightful Scottish countryside are close at hand. *Directions:* From Perth take the A9 (Inverness) to the A827 to Aberfeldy where you take the B846 through Ween. Farlayer House is on you right shortly after Castle Menzies.

FARLAYER HOUSE
Owners: Francis & Bill Atkins
Aberfeldy
Perthshire PH5 2JE
tel (0887) 20332 fax (0887) 29430
11 rooms
Single from £85, Double from £160
  (Dinner, B & B)
Open all year
Credit cards: all major
Children welcome

Ardvasar Hotel is a traditional, no frills, country pub that has gained a reputation for good Scottish food.   Bill Fowler loves to cook and changes his set dinner menu every evening depending upon what is fresh and locally available.   He always offers a choice of starters and a choice of fish, poultry, and meat for the main course.   Overnight guests have the use of a simply furnished lounge for relaxing and enjoying after-dinner coffee.   If you are in the mood to meet locals and other visitors to the Isle of Skye, you can go into the adjacent pub.   Bedrooms are not fancy in their decor and vary in size from small to quite large family rooms. Nearby is the Clan Donald Centre where an audiovisual program and exhibits give an overview of Skye's turbulent clan history.   Highlights of a driving tour around Skye are Portree, Skye Cottage Museum, Talisker Distillery, Dunvegan Castle, and (if the weather is clear) stupendous views of wild scenery with the sea ever in the background.   *Directions:*   Ardvasar Hotel is located just a short drive from the Mallaig to Arndale ferry at the southern tip of the Isle of Skye.   Although the crossing takes less than an hour, it is a long, cumbersome procedure to load and unload cars onto and off the boat.   As an alternative you can take the fast, very short ferry ride from Kyle of Lochalsh (for which no reservations are needed) and enjoy the hour's drive to Ardvasar.

ARDVASAR HOTEL
Owners: Greta & Bill Fowler
Ardvasar
Isle of Skye IV45 8RS
tel (04714) 223
10 rooms
From £30 per person B & B
Open March to November
Credit cards: MC VS
Children welcome

The Reid family, wealthy industrialists who built steam locomotives, had a yen for grandeur when they built Auchterarder in the 1830s as their country residence.   It boasts vast rooms with lofty ceilings, lavishly panelled halls and reception rooms, and a winter garden conservatory leading to an ornate sitting room--a tremendous amount of craftsmanship went into this magnificent house.   This is truly a house of the age of Scottish baronial architecture, an era of grandeur which the Browns have gone to great lengths to keep and enhance with the use of ornate wallpapers and elaborate furnishings.   This is very much a family operation: two sons are chefs, a daughter-in-law supervises the restaurant, while Audrey and Ian concentrate on making guests feel at home.   The six very large master bedrooms have high ceilings, tall windows, and very spacious bathrooms.   The Graham Room has a particularly impressive array of fitted furniture.   The Stuart Room sports a huge Victorian bathroom with marble floor and walls and a large clawfoot tub with a dinner-plate sized shower head.   Turret and courtyard rooms are, by comparison, small rooms with much quieter decor.   Perth, the ancient capital of Scotland, is only a few miles away, as are Stirling Castle, Drummond Castle, and Crief. *Directions:* From Perth take the A9 (Stirling road) to Auchterarder where you turn right on the Crief road.   The hotel is on your right after 1 1/2 miles.

AUCHTERARDER HOUSE
Owners: Audrey & Ian Brown
Auchterarder
Perthshire PH3 1DZ
tel (0764) 63646   fax (0764) 62939
15 rooms
Single from £85, Double from £125
Open all year
Credit cards: all major
Children over 10

Stewart and Sheila Spence had long dreamed of creating a luxurious country house hotel near Aberdeen, so in their extensive travels they garnered ideas from the lovely places they stayed. When they settled on Invery House as being just the kind of small Georgian mansion they wanted, they put their plans into action and spared no expense in creating this luxury hotel, one of the most sought-after in Scotland. Exquisite antique furniture and elegant decor are the order of the day here. Everything is bright and shining and of the highest standard. The bedrooms and bathrooms are kitted out with almost every pampering extra you can think of--thick bathrobes, a decanter of sherry, and, in several cases, large sunken tubs in bathrooms almost as large as the bedrooms themselves. A grand billiard room graces the basement alongside the wine cellar which offers choices from over 400 different wines. The chef prides himself on food of the very highest standards. Nearby Aberdeen, once a fishing port, is now a bustling oil-boom town. For excellent sightseeing, follow the A93 through Royal Deeside to Aboyne with its historic castle, and Ballater to the royal home of Balmoral and on to Braemar. *Directions:* From Aberdeen take the A93 to Banchory, turn left towards Fettercairn and the hotel driveway is on your left shortly after you pass the Bridge of Feugh.

INVERY HOUSE
Owners: Sheila & Stewart Spence
Bridge of Feugh
Banchory
Kincardineshire AB3 3NJ
tel (03302) 4782 fax (03302) 4712
14 rooms
Single from £85, Double from £95
Open all year
Credit cards: all major
Children over 8

Isolated by its own private, liberally wooded grounds, the Raemoir House Hotel is a large, sheltered Georgian mansion. A Scottish sporting hotel, it offers fishing, shooting, and deer stalking. Being a large home with high ceilings and wide passages, it is able to carry grand pieces of furniture. Surrounded by dark wood panelling in the drawing room, guests gather to enjoy drinks and quiet conversation before dinner in the dining room, which is elegant and spacious. There are also a number of lounges for after-dinner coffee or liqueurs, or where you can relax in the fading afternoons and watch the sun's shadows melt away. Bedrooms are not luxurious but come in all shapes and sizes and are liberally furnished with interesting antiques. Several rooms are in an adjacent 15th-century house or across the lawn in the converted stables. All ages of children are most welcome-- the hotel has everything from babysitters to games and toys. Kit Sabin, now ably assisted by daughter Judy, son-in-law Mike, and their daughter Nikki, extends a warmth of welcome which makes the hotel special: her warm smile, sense of humor, and love of her home add to the enjoyment of a stay here. There are many fine castles to visit in this area: Crathes, Drum, Aboyne, and Balmoral. *Directions:* From Aberdeen take the A93 (Perth road) to Banchory, then turn right on the A980 (Raemoir road) for the 2 1/2-mile drive to Raemoir House.

RAEMOIR HOUSE HOTEL
Owners: Kit Sabin & family
Banchory
Grampian AB31 4ED
tel (03302) 4884   fax (03302) 2171
22 rooms
Single from £60, Double from £100
Closed for 2 weeks in January
Credit cards: all major
Children welcome

Californian hospitality, a historical building dating back to 1199, good food, roaring fires, and lots of comfort epitomize Shieldhill. The owners, Jack Greenwald, a Californian, and Christine Dunstan, originally from England, have combined their talents to create this lovely hotel. Christine has done the most exquisite job with the eye-catching decor: a different color has been used in each of the public rooms-- a muted red in the mahogany-panelled sitting room, a vivid blue in the upstairs drawing room. The bedrooms, each in a different Laura Ashley print, are named after famous Scottish battles, with the exception of the Chancellor Suite, named for the Chancellors who lived at Shieldhill from 1560 to 1959. This enormous bedroom, a touch of California in Scotland, has a king sized bed and a jacuzzi tub that fits four. If your tastes run to more traditional country house bedchambers, they are here aplenty: three have four-poster beds, two have jacuzzi tubs, all have either queen or king sized beds, immaculate bathrooms with showers, and one has a resident ghost. Fresh fruit, homemade shortbread, and a decanter of sherry all help make the guest feel happy and pampered. Shieldhill is an ideal base to explore the border towns and to visit Edinburgh and Glasgow which are less than an hours drive away. *Directions:* Shieldhill is 5 miles east of Biggar on the A721.

SHIELDHILL HOTEL
Owners: Christine Dunstan & Jack Greenwald
Quothquan
Biggar
Lanarkshire ML12 6NA
tel (0899) 20035 fax (0899) 21092
11 rooms
Single from £88, Double from £98
Closed January
Credit cards: all major
Children over 12

Braemar Lodge is a most attractive small hotel run by Marion and Trevor Campbell. Marion loves to cook, changing the menu every day, and you can look forward to a meal that can vary between a two-course dinner and a five-course feast. Beyond the attractive dining room and homey sitting room, a small panelled bar with a blazing log fire is the focal point of this delightful hotel. Upstairs the bedrooms with their fresh paint and light colors are most attractive. Five have en-suite bathrooms with showers while two smaller bedrooms share a bathroom with a tub. On the first Saturday in September, Scotland's most famous Highland Games, the Braemar Gathering, draws thousands to the spectacle of kilted clansmen, pipe bands, caber tossing, and the like. If you book a year in advance, Braemar Lodge can offer you accommodation within walking distance of the games. But do not confine your visit to Braemar to this one famous week--the area around Braemar has much to offer: golf on the highest golf course in Scotland, Balmoral, the nearby home of the Royal Family, fishing, skiing (at nearby Glenshee), and the mountains and castles of the Scottish Highlands. *Directions:* Braemar is on the A93, 50 miles northwest of Perth.

BRAEMAR LODGE HOTEL
Owners: Marion and Trevor Campbell
Braemar
Aberdeenshire AB3 5YQ
tel (03397) 41627
7 rooms
From £27.50 per person B & B
Closed November, December & April
Credit cards: MC VS
Children welcome

Callander is a delightful, small Scottish town, the gateway to the Trossachs, a lovely area of mountains and lochs.   Situated just off the town's main street, its large garden bordering the banks of the River Teith, the Roman Camp remains one of my favorite Scottish hotels.   The building's pale pink walls and small, gray-roofed turrets create a charming atmosphere that is continued indoors.   It is the feel of this lovely hotel with its stately, dark panelled library and comfortable sitting room rather than its elegant decor that endears it to me.   Eric Brown, who grew up in Callander, his wife, Marion, and their young, friendly staff offer a warm Scottish welcome.   Dinner is served in the long, slender dining room under its low, ornately painted ceiling.   Long corridors and narrow winding staircases lead to the bedrooms which come in all shapes and sizes, fitting into the rooms of the old house, the adjacent cottage, and extensions that have been added over the years. A walk through woodlands along the bank of the River Teith brings you into Callander with its little shops and gray stone houses stretched out along the road. Nearby are the Trossachs and their lovely lakes, Loch Katrine, Loch Achray, and Loch Venachar.   *Directions:* Callander is only an hour's drive from Edinburgh. Take the M9 to junction 10, beyond Stirling, and the A84 towards Crianlarich. You will find the entrance to Roman Camp on the main street of town.

ROMAN CAMP HOTEL
Owners: Marion & Eric Brown
Callander
Perthshire FK17 8BG
tel (0877) 30003 fax (0877) 31533
14 rooms
Single from £80, Double from £90
Open all year
Credit cards: all major
Children welcome

If you are coming to Loch Ness to look for Nessie or simply to spend some time in the tranquility of the Highlands, there can be no better place to stay than Polmaily House. This large Victorian home is now a hotel of great character run by Nicholas and Alison Parsons. It's one of those wonderful places where everything has a homey feel to it--the overstuffed chintz chairs beckoned a particular welcome after a busy day sightseeing. Little tables decked with blue and white tablecloths and topped with simple country flower arrangements make the dining room a most inviting place and set the casual tone for the scrumptious dinners that Alison Parsons prepares. The menu is a la carte and changes daily. Most of the vegetables and all of the herbs come fresh from the garden. The very nicest bedrooms are 1, 2, and 4, large rooms that enjoy lovely views to the front of the house. The smallest rooms are the two singles that share a bathroom. An outdoor swimming pool is there for any who dare brave its icy waters: the tennis court and croquet lawn see far more activity than the pool. The Monster Research Centre is nearby. You can explore beautiful Glen Affric, visit Culloden battlefield where Bonnie Prince Charlie led his Highlanders into hopeless battle, and Cawdor Castle, scene of Duncan's murder in *Macbeth*. *Directions:* From Drumnadrochit take the A831 towards Cannich and Polmaily House is on your right after 2 miles.

POLMAILY HOUSE
Owners: Alison & Nick Parsons
Drumnadrochit
Inverness-shire IV3 6XT
tel (04562) 343
9 rooms
Single from £45, Double from £100
Open April to mid-October
Credit cards: MC VS
Children welcome

The tree-lined drive winds through a vast estate to the parklike lawns surrounding Cromlix House. Little rabbits hop gaily around, so tame that you can approach within a few yards of them before they disappear into the surrounding woodlands. The heavy, unattractive Victorian exterior of Cromlix House hides a jewel of an interior. Converted in 1981 from the Eden family home, the original Victorian bedroom and reception room furniture has been retained along with the exquisite family porcelain, heavy silver, and glassware that grace the lovely dining rooms. The tone of an elegant Victorian home is set by the stately front hall with its wooden ceiling and richly panelled walls and is carried through into the inviting drawing rooms, peaceful, well-stocked library, and garden conservatory. Unusual features are the gun room, the private chapel with its organ pipes gracing one of the staircases, and the way the set five-course dinner is verbally offered to you and choices discussed should you not care for the meal that is proposed. Upstairs are 14 large and very comfortable bedrooms, 8 of which are suites, all with spacious bathrooms. Within a half-hour drive are the Trossachs and their lovely lakes, Stirling Castle, and Bannockburn. *Directions:* Take the A9 out of Dunblane, turn left onto B8033, go through Kinbuck village and take the second left turn after a small bridge.

CROMLIX HOUSE
Owners: Victoria & Edward Eden
Kinbuck by Dunblane
Perthshire FK15 9JT
tel (0786) 822125 fax (0786) 825450
14 rooms
Single from £100, Double from £125
Open all year
Credit cards: all major
Children welcome

Kinnaird was built in 1770 as a home on the vast Atholl Estate.   In 1990 Constance Ward turned her home into a hotel, keeping all its grandeur and the hospitality that characterized her and her late husband's sporting house parties.   John Webber, a distinguished chef, joined Mrs Ward in the venture as chef and manager.   From a large entrance hall you enter the Cedar Room, an elegant, comfortable, cedar-panelled sitting room with a door opening onto a grand billiard room--your first clue that Kinnaird is a sporting estate as well as a luxury hotel.   The quality of everything from the furniture to gorgeous fabrics and decor (much of it in shades of green) is a delight.   The dining room with its delicately painted panelwork and stunning views of the Tay valley is a gorgeous.   The same quality of good taste extends to the spacious bedrooms, many of which are furnished with antiques or copies of furniture originally in the house.   Acres of lawns and shrubbery lead to the vast sporting estate.   Sportsmen have a comfortable, clubby sitting room below stairs where they can bring their dogs.   A short distance away lies Dunkeld with its ruined cathedral, a most attractive town as are Crieff and Bridge of Cally. *Directions:* From Perth take the A9 towards Inverness.   Pass Dunkeld and take the B898 towards Dalguise.   After 4 miles the gates of Kinnaird are on your right.

KINNAIRD
Owner: Constance Ward
Chef-Manager: John Webber
Kinnaird Estate by Dunkeld
Perthshire PH8 0LB
tel (079) 682440   fax (079) 682289
9 rooms
Single from £91, Double from £130
Closed February
Credit cards: all major
Children over 12

The location is absolutely perfect--just a ten-minute stroll from Princes Street in the heart of Georgian Edinburgh, three townhouses have been joined to form this exquisite luxury hotel which has the air of a private club. Within, no expense has been spared to create the look and feel of a sumptuous home. Beautiful fabrics, antiques, gorgeous furniture, and lots of flowers set an elegant mood. The drawing room, decked out in dark colors with wing-back chairs and a plump sofa drawn round the fireplace sets the masculine tone for the hotel, though it is not a dark or dreary place. There is no bar: guests order from the waiter. Each bedroom has a different luxurious decor and color scheme. A great many of the bathrooms are especially grand, marble affairs with sparkling chrome fittings. Edinburgh abounds with restaurants from formal to funky--if the former is to your taste, you can do no better than Number 36, the hotel's basement restaurant where high-backed green paisley chairs, red tartan tablecloths overlaid with white linen, panelled walls, and intimate dining nooks create a delightful atmosphere. Park your car in the hotel's off-street car park and explore this lovely town on foot. The Howard is within strolling distance of Princes Street with its shops and stores and the Castle. *Directions:* From Princes Street (with the castle on your left) turn right on Hanover and Great King Street is the fourth road on your right.

THE HOWARD
Manager: Christopher Sharp
32-36 Great King Street
Edinburgh EH3 6QN
tel (031) 5573500 fax (031) 5576515
16 rooms
Single from £97, Double from £148
Open all year
Credit cards: all major
Children welcome

A long, tree-lined drive leads to Prestonfield House Hotel, located beyond the city suburbs in a countryside setting just ten minutes' drive from the center of Edinburgh.   An elegant mood is set by peacocks strutting gracefully on a circular lawn directly in front of this grand, white stone manor (sometimes they provide unrequested early wake-up calls).   The hotel's interior is delightfully dignified and old-fashioned.   Its old wood floors are warmed by attractive rugs; oil paintings and tapestries dress the thick walls; archways frame intimate sitting areas; soft lighting and scattered flower arrangements add gentle touches.   You dine in the almost circular restaurant watched over by massive portraits of long dead ancestors. After dinner you climb a worn stone staircase to the dignified tapestry room where, beneath the most ornate of plasterwork ceilings, little groups of tables and chairs are set for coffee, chocolates, and after-dinner drinks.   In keeping with the public rooms, the bedrooms have a very old-fashioned feel to them.   Bruce and Cunningham have en-suite bathrooms, while the smaller bedrooms share two bathrooms.   A continental breakfast is served in the bedrooms.   From April to October a "Taste of Scotland" evening with dinner, song, dance, and, of course, bagpipes is held in the adjacent stables.   *Directions:* From the city center take the A68 (A7).   Turn left at the lights after passing the Commonwealth swimming pool.

PRESTONFIELD HOUSE HOTEL
Owners: The Stevenson family
Priestfield Road
Edinburgh EH16 5UT
tel (031) 6683346   fax (031) 6683976
5 rooms
Single from £43, Double from £74
Open all year
Credit cards: all major
Children welcome

For those who wish they could afford to stay at Inverlochy Castle with Grete Hobbs, perhaps the next best thing to staying there is to stay next door with her son, Peter Hobbs, at The Factor's House.   Guests can walk through the extensive grounds to the castle and may use the tennis courts and fish in the loch.   Peter has taken what was once the estate manager's (factor's) house and enlarged and modernized it, creating a small, modern, welcoming hotel that is very different from his mother's elegant establishment.   A homey mixture of sofas and chairs graces the main lounge and a blackboard outlines the dinner menu and any special activities available for guests that day.   Pancho, a sleek black labrador, is usually on hand to ensure that he gets an appropriate amount of attention.   In the evening it's a cheerful, relaxed kind of place as guests gather for drinks and conversation and select records to play on the stereo.   The dining room offers a short set menu as well as the daily specials.   Upstairs the bedrooms have a most attractive pastel decor and are well equipped with television, telephone, and spotless modern bathrooms.   Popular sights include Loch Ness to catch a glimpse of its monster and the Glenfinnan monument to Bonnie Prince Charlie at the head of Loch Sheil. *Directions:* The Factor's House is 3 miles out of Fort William on the A82 Inverness road, on the left.

THE FACTOR'S HOUSE
Owner: Peter Hobbs
Torlundy by Fort William
Inverness-shire PH33 6SN
tel (0397) 705767 fax (0397) 702953
7 rooms
Single from £75, Double from £85
Open mid-March to mid-November
Credit cards: MC VS
Children over 6

Under the attentive eye of the owner, Grete Hobbs, Inverlochy Castle remains Scotland's premier luxury hotel. This Highland home of the Hobbs family is screened from the main road by a winding driveway and groves of rhododendrons. Surrounded by landscaped gardens overlooking its own private loch, the turreted and gabled house was built to resemble a castle. Its magnificence does not appear to have altered since Queen Victoria visited in 1873. In her diaries she wrote, "I never saw a lovelier nor more romantic spot." Central heating and modern plumbing appear to be the only 20th-century additions. The two-storied Grand Hall with its frescoed ceiling sets the tone of this memorable hotel and the furnishings and decor throughout are luxurious. Dinners in the elaborate dining room are elegant affairs. The staff outnumber the guests and attention to detail ensures that things are done properly. The small number of rooms and the hotel's popularity mean that early reservations are necessary. Inverlochy Castle is very grand, very expensive, and the most outstanding hotel. From Fort William you can take the Road to the Isles, a lovely, dead-end drive that brings you to Mallaig where you can take ferries to the isles of Skye, Rhum, Eigg, Canna, and Muck. *Directions:* The castle is on the A82, Inverness road, 3 miles north of Fort William.

INVERLOCHY CASTLE
Manager: Michael Leonard
Torlundy
Fort William
Inverness-shire PH33 6SN
tel (0397) 702177 fax (0397) 702953
16 rooms
Single from £140, Double from £175
Open mid-March to mid-November
Credit cards: all major
Children welcome

Just a five-minute drive from the center of Glasgow in a fashionable Victorian suburb, three adjacent grand Victorian mansions, once the homes of wealthy industrialists, are now a funky, luxury hotel. As the name suggests, the hotel began in number 1 and has since been joined by 2 and 3. The houses are not interconnected, so you pop in and out, under wide umbrellas when it's raining-- dining rooms are in 1, reception, drawing room, and bar in 3. Spectacular features of 2 and 3 are the enormous, two-story stained glass windows half-way up the staircases. Bedrooms are for the most part very large and high-ceilinged. Our attic room was large enough for a sofa and easy chairs as well as a dining room table and chairs--a gorgeously decorated twin room in blue/gray silk. A great many of the rooms have four-posters swathed in countless yards of striking, dark colored fabric--one room is done completely in black. Number 3 has the quietest, most traditional decor. The layers of grime are gone from Glasgow's solid Victorian buildings, revealing honey-colored architectural masterpieces. The Burrell Collection houses the largest private art collection in Britain. *Directions:* Leave the M8 at junction 17 onto the Great Western Road which you follow to Hyndland Road. Turn left and first right three times which brings you to the hotel.

ONE DEVONSHIRE GARDENS
Owner: Ken McCullough
Manager: Beverly Payne
Devonshire Gardens
Glasgow G12 0UX
tel (041) 3392001 fax (041) 3371663
27 rooms
Single from £110, Double from £125
Open all year
Credit cards: all major
Children welcome

On an estate of 22,000 acres, Tulchan Lodge is beautifully positioned overlooking the Spey Valley. Tastefully elegant with grand accommodations, refined service, and excellent food and wines, Tulchan Lodge is an exquisite Edwardian sporting lodge set in the Highlands of Scotland. The warm atmosphere created by groupings of comfortable chairs and sofas around blazing log fires in the hall and lounges extends to the library, billiards room, and dining rooms. The luxury continues in the bedrooms with their good antique furniture, colorful matching fabrics for the bedcovers, chairs and curtains, and panoramic views of the River Spey and its valley. This sportsman's paradise offers salmon and sea trout fishing on the Spey, grouse shooting on the heather-clad moors, varied and exciting low ground shooting in the valleys, and roe deer stalking. The entire lodge can be booked exclusively for a party of up to 22 persons. Guests making a non-sporting visit will be enchanted by the sparkling mountain rivers, open moorlands (Culloden Battlefield is well worth a visit), pine forests, ancient castles (Balmoral, Cawdor, Blair, and Craigievar), rugged coastline, and the distilleries on the Speyside Malt Whiskey Trail. *Directions:* From Grantown-on-Spey take the A939 (Nairn road) for a short distance, turning right on the B9102 to Tulchan Lodge near Advie.

TULCHAN LODGE
Estate Factor: Mr T. J. Kirkwood
Advie by Grantown-on-Spey
Moray PH26 3PW
tel (08075) 200/261 fax (08075) 234
11 rooms
From £170 per person, dinner, B & B
Open for individuals mid-April to September
Open for shooting parties October to January
Credit cards: none
Children welcome

Golf players will be enchanted with Greywalls because it is on the very edge of the Great Muirfield golf course founded in 1744. Even if you have no interest in the game, you will love this most beautiful of houses built in 1901 by Sir Edward Lutyens and you will adore the gardens laid out like a series of rooms by Gertrude Jekyll. It was the Weaver family home until 1948 when they turned it into a hotel--family photos and letters decorate the ladies loo (perhaps they also adorn the gents--I did not visit) and photos of famous guests, particularly golfers, are grouped around the reception area. The dining room overlooks the 10th green. The lounges are especially attractive, particularly the panelled library with its interesting pictures, shelves of books, and open fireplace. The bar is most convivial. Edward VII used to stay here and, because he admired the view, a special outside loo-with-a-view was built for him near the garden wall: now it's a suite called King's Loo. Guests can choose it or from an array of bedrooms that overlook either the flower-filled gardens or the golf course. A Monday or Friday golf package can be arranged in conjunction with a two-night stay, though guests can make their own arrangements at Muirfield as well as at the other ten courses nearby. Eighteen miles to the west lies Edinburgh. *Directions:* From Edinburgh take the A1 to the A198, go through Gullane and the hotel is on your left.

GREYWALLS
Owners: Ros & Giles Weaver
Muirfield by Gullane
East Lothian EH31 2EG
tel (0620) 842144 fax (0620) 842241
23 rooms
Single from £80, Double from £125
Closed February
Credit cards: all major
Children welcome

Dunain Park Hotel is a lovely country home overlooking the famous Caledonian Canal which joins Loch Ness to the Murray Firth. The large sitting room with its crackling log fire provides a snug retreat on stormy days. Anne Nicoll loves to cook, using vegetables from the garden and lamb, beef, venison, and salmon fresh from local suppliers and mixing traditional Scottish cooking with modern continental. The choice bedrooms are in the main house and another three occupy a little cottage on the edge of the walled vegetable garden. Room 1 overlooks the back garden and has an elegant, four-poster canopy bed and a delicate writing desk tucked into one corner. Room 5 has a handsome, light-wood Victorian half-tester bed and lovely views of the grounds. All the guestrooms are papered with rather bright, flowery wallpapers. (Recently a new wing of 6 suites has been added--larger rooms with a separate sitting room which can be used as a second bedroom.) A log chalet houses a heated swimming pool and sauna. Inverness is a very pleasant town with a superb theatre, Eden Court. A very pleasant drive is around Loch Ness to Fort Augustus and back on the other bank. The Monster Research Centre is on the north bank near Drumnadrochit. *Directions:* Dunain Park Hotel is just off the A82, 2 miles south of Inverness.

DUNAIN PARK HOTEL
Owners: Anne & Edward Nicoll
Dunain Park
by Inverness
Inverness-shire IV3 6JN
tel (0463) 230512 fax (0463) 224532
14 rooms
Double from £110
Open all year
Credit cards: all major
Children welcome

Set in the Border Country, Sunlaws House Hotel provides visitors driving to or from England with an ideal base for exploring the eastern Scottish Lowlands. The rambling Victorian house with its large sunny rooms is surrounded by a spacious garden of rolling lawns and trees. From their residence at nearby Floors Castle, the owners, the Duke and Duchess of Roxburgh, supervised the conversion of Sunlaws in 1982 from a private home to a hotel, chose the decor, and provided much of the fine antique furniture that graces this charming country hotel. Sports enthusiasts will enjoy the excellent fishing in the nearby Tweed. Tennis and croquet are available within the grounds. For those who just wish to relax, the large conservatory, inviting lounge, and panelled library (which is also the bar) provide ideal locations. A skylit staircase leads to the large comfortable bedrooms. My favorite bedrooms are Room 10 with its large bay window framing a lovely view, and Room 8 with its large windows and balcony. Floors Castle, a vast, very ornate home, is the largest lived-in home in Scotland. By contrast Tranquair House is Scotland's oldest home, dating from 950--this is a must-visit home and the tour is both educational and fun. *Directions:* From Kelso take the A698 towards Heiton: Sunlaws House is signposted 3 miles out of town.

SUNLAWS HOUSE HOTEL
Manager: David Corkill
Sunlaws by Kelso
Roxburghshire TD5 8JZ
tel (05735) 331 fax (05735) 611
22 rooms
Single from £62, Double from £82
Open all year
Credit cards: all major
Children welcome

Overlooking the romantic ruins of Kildrummy Castle and surrounded by acres of lovely gardens and woodlands, Kildrummy Castle Hotel is a grand mansion house. The richly panelled and tapestried walls and ornately carved staircase give a baronial feel to this grand house, a feel that is echoed in the lounge and bar whose large windows overlook the romantic castle ruins and the gardens.   Yet this is not a stuffy, formal hotel: the smiling, friendly staff do a splendid job, offering people a warmth of welcome that was unsurpassed by any other on my most recent visit to Scotland.   Dinner in the richly furnished dining room is a delight.   The bedrooms (named after various pools in the hotel's trout stream) are tastefully decorated and traditionally furnished.   Their size ranges from a snug attic bedroom with a private balcony to a grand corner room with enormous windows framing the countryside. From Kildrummy you can join the Speyside Whisky Trail and enjoy a wee dram. At Alford lies Craigievar, a fairytale castle unchanged since it was built in 1626. Nearby Ballater is a busy resort surrounded by wooded hills.   Between Kildrummy and Braemar, home of the September Royal Highland Gathering, lies Balmoral Castle whose grounds are open in July and August when the Royal Family is not in residence.   *Directions:* From Aberdeen take the A944 through Alford to the A97 where you turn left for Kildrummy Castle.

KILDRUMMY CASTLE HOTEL
Owner: Thomas Hanna
Kildrummy by Alford
Aberdeenshire AB3 8RA
tel (03365) 288
17 rooms
Single from £35, Double from £72
Closed January and February
Credit cards: all major
Children welcome

Ballathie House is a large, turreted, Victorian Scottish country estate home on the banks of the River Tay, surrounded by lawns, fields, and woodlands. With its riverside location, salmon fishing is a big attraction, while golf is an ever-popular pastime. David Assenti manages the hotel and has done a stupendous job redecorating and refurbishing this lovely old house. The entrance hall, dining room, and lounges are spacious rooms. Rooms are graded according to size and view into master, superior, and standard accommodation. My favorites are the spacious bedrooms with turret bathrooms and the smaller rooms with river views. There is a ground floor suite, equipped for the handicapped, beyond the kitchen. The bar was a lively place and dinner was delicious with friendly, efficient service. Nearby is Dunkeld, a delightful town with a ruined cathedral set in expansive lawns. Scone Palace, where Scottish kings were once crowned, has fine furniture, clocks, porcelain, and needlework. *Directions:* From Perth take the A9 towards Inverness for about 10 minutes to the B9099, Stanley road. Go through Stanley and take a righthand fork towards Blairgowrie, following signs for Ballathie House.

BALLATHIE HOUSE
Manager: David Assenti
Kinclaven
near Perth
Perthshire PH1 4QN
tel (025083) 268 fax (025083) 396
27 rooms
Single from £83, Double from £150
* Dinner, B & B*
Closed February
Credit cards: all major
Children welcome

Glenscripesdale House is farther away from civilization than any other hotel in this guide and everything that is served to you is either brought in by boat or bounced down 9 miles of dirt track. Electricity comes from the log-fired generator, the phone is on a radio link, and mail is collected from across the loch. There are no extras added to your bill: breakfast, a packed lunch, dinner, endless pots of tea and coffee are all included--along with the occasional load of washing for longer-staying guests--few stay just overnight. It's all very comfortable, informal, and friendly. The snug, book-lined sitting room is full of homey furniture and packed with novels, games, and information for tramping the countryside. At dinner Sue cooks and Bill helps guests choose a wine. Families are welcome--children can play dress-up and table tennis in the hay loft if the weather is inclement. Up the narrow staircase are two floors of bedrooms on either side of a landing. Bedroom 1 is a particularly large twin with a Victorian tub in the bathroom. An extra bedroom is found beyond the laundry and pantry. Guests go walking, fishing, and explore the inlets and islands of the loch by boat--Bill conducts expeditions in the rubber inflatable or guests can go out, map in hand, in the small green dinghy. *Directions:* Glenscripesdale House is about 36 miles from Fort William. While you cannot fax to the hotel, they have a service which can fax driving directions to you.

GLENSCRIPESDALE HOUSE
Owners: Sue & Bill Hemmings
Loch Sunart (Acharacle)
Argyll PH36 4JH
tel (096785) 263
4 rooms
From £55 per person, dinner, lunch, B & B
Closed November to March
   (except for Xmas & New Year)
Credit cards: none
Children welcome

Clifton House is a unique hotel which reflects the character of its owners, the Gordon MacIntyre family, and their love of the theatre. As a highlight during the winter months, from October to May, a number of plays, concerts, and recitals are staged in the hotel. The overall decor is flamboyantly Victorian, abounding in flowers, masses of pictures, rich colors, and draped curtains. A log fire lures you into the warmth of the main lounge with its ornate, hand-blocked wallpaper that was used in the robing room of the Palace of Westminster in 1849--it is very loud and marvelously Victorian. Each of the 16 bedrooms has its own flavor and personality, and one must appreciate the imagination and interest behind each individual scheme. The bedrooms tend to be decorated dramatically, so it is as well to ask to see several rooms to decide which suits you best. Small, artistic, and colorful, the Clifton is personally managed by the family members and a very conscientious staff. Clifton House is interesting and fun to stay in. Nairn is an old fishing/seaside town on the Moray Firth. There are several castles to visit (Cawdor, Brodie, Balvenie, and Grant) and whisky distilleries to tour. *Directions:* From Inverness take the A96 (15 miles) to Nairn, turn left at the only roundabout in town and Clifton House is on your left after half a mile.

CLIFTON HOUSE
Owner: Gordon MacIntyre
Viewfield Street
Nairn
Nairnshire IV12 4HW
tel (0667) 53119 fax (0667) 52836
16 rooms
Single from £50, Double from £100
Open February to November
Credit cards: all major
Children welcome

The Peat Inn has for many years had an international reputation for outstanding cooking which has won for David Wilson a coveted Michelin star and Chef Laureate from the British Gastronomic Academy. The surrounding village is so small that it is appropriately called Peat Inn after the inn. Surrounded by miles of fields and farmlands, it seems an unlikely spot for a world-class restaurant, but diners come from far and wide to indulge their palates and their eyes with exquisite food. After dinner patrons simply walk across the courtyard to the purpose-built Residence where eight suites (all but one identical in design) offer luxurious accommodation with a small sitting room upstairs and a bedroom and bathroom downstairs. Each bedroom is sumptuously appointed with king, double, or twin beds. I much preferred the "odd man out," a very spacious bedroom/sitting room on one level overlooking the garden. A continental breakfast of fruit and breads is served in the room. While the rooms are lovely, the undoubted reason for coming here is to dine. The Peat Inn is just 6 miles from the home of golf, St Andrews. Edinburgh is an hour's drive away, Dundee half an hour. *Directions:* Peat Inn is at the junction of the B940 and the B941, 6 miles east of Cupar and 6 miles southwest of St Andrews.

THE PEAT INN
Owners: Patricia & David Wilson
Peat Inn
by Cupar
Fife KY15 5LH
tel (033484) 206 fax (033484) 530
8 suites
Single from £95, Double from £115
Closed Sunday & Monday
Credit cards: all major
Children over 10

This turreted, baronial-style mansion stands on the site of the home of Colonel Alexander Murray who accepted the surrender of Quebec after General Wolfe was killed. A traditional lounge bar is the only ground-floor room, the gracious, panelled drawing room and spacious dining room being found up the dramatic, sweeping staircase. In recent years the Maguires have replaced the worn hallway and stair carpets with an exact match of the old one in a vibrant, bright plum color-- some question their decision. Bedrooms are all over the place--in attics, beyond the kitchens, up the main staircase, up the back service stairs. They come in all shapes and sizes, have the same tariff, and modern bathrooms. The old-fashioned lift is useful for those who have difficulty with stairs. Stanley and son Simon deal with the front of the house (Simon is passionate about hens) while mother Aileen supervises the kitchen with son Paul (who is passionate about beekeeping). The food is especially good and attracts a great deal of local patronage. In the grounds are beautiful, lush, green lawns and flowerbeds leading to a bountiful, walled vegetable garden. The ancient abbeys, remote castles, and small wool towns of the Tweed Valley that lie just a few miles to the south of Edinburgh can easily be explored from Cringletie House Hotel. *Directions:* Cringletie House is on the A703, 3 miles north of Peebles and 20 miles south of Edinburgh.

CRINGLETIE HOUSE HOTEL
Owners: The Maguire family
Peebles
Peeblesshire EH45 8PL
tel (07213) 233
13 rooms
Single from £44, Double from £80
Open mid-March to January 2nd
Credit cards: MC VS
Children welcome

Surrounded by the peace and quiet of the countryside yet only a few minutes' drive from the center of Pitlochry, Auchnahyle is a complex of cottages and farm buildings set round a farmyard. The largest cottage is Penny and Alistair's home and inside everything is cottage-cozy, brimming with a charming array of antiques. A snug dining room and lounge open off either side of the steep narrow staircase that leads to the two little bedrooms with rambling roses peeping in at the windows. These share a central bathroom--if the snug, twin room downstairs is booked and you request a private bathroom, Alistair will see that the other bedroom remains unoccupied. Penny cooks as though she is giving a private dinner party and guests are encouraged to bring their own wine. Across the farmyard Rowan Tree Cottage is rented for family vacations: parents often tuck their children in bed and slip across the farmyard for a meal. Two friendly dogs, So-So and Waggle, goats, and an aged donkey complete the rural picture. Pitlochry is a delightful town absolutely stuffed with woolen shops--you can spend a day just choosing a selection of sweaters. The Festival Theatre is a great draw and Blair Castle is only a 10-minute drive away. *Directions:* Enter Pitlochry from the south (A9). Pass under the railway bridge, turn right on East Moulin Road and take the fourth turning right (by letter box). Continue bearing right until you reach Auchnahyle.

AUCHNAHYLE
Owners: Penny & Alistair Howman
Pitlochry
Perthshire PH16 5JA
tel (0796) 2318 fax (0796) 3657
3 rooms
From £27 per person B & B
Open Easter to October
Credit cards: VS
Children over 12

Pitlochry developed in the latter half of the 19th century as a Highland health resort and remains today an attractive town of sturdy Victorian houses standing back from the wooded shores of Loch Faskally. Knockendarroch House stands above the rooftops of the town, isolated by its own little hill and surrounding garden. Mary and John, having launched a family of six children, now devote themselves to taking care of their guests. Their tremendous enthusiasm and warmth really contribute to the hotel. Guests who wish to dine are treated to a glass of sherry as they peruse the three-course dinner menu. Intertwining flowers decorate the stained glass windows which filter sunlight onto the staircase leading up to the spacious, high-ceilinged bedrooms--2 of the snug attic bedrooms have little balconies overlooking the rooftops of the town. All are crisply decorated and equipped with color television, coffee, and tea makings and have modern bathrooms with showers. If you have difficulty with stairs you will appreciate the ground-floor bedroom. Pitlochry and the surrounding countryside has much to keep visitors occupied for several days. During the summer season the Pitlochry Festival Theatre has a repertoire of plays which makes it possible for you to see as many as four plays in a three-night stay. *Directions:* Pitlochry is 28 miles north of Perth on the A9.

KNOCKENDARROCH HOUSE
Owners: Mary & John McMenemie
Higher Oakfield
Pitlochry
Perthshire PH16 5HT
tel (0796) 3473
12 rooms
From £32 per person B & B
Open April to October
Credit cards: all major
Children welcome

The Airds Hotel, a long, low, white ferry inn, looks down on the shore of Loch Linnhe, the Isle of Lismore, and the green Morvern Mountains. Eric and Betty Allen have converted this delightful hostelry into an intimate country house hotel that provides a haven of perfect tranquility in a stunningly beautiful area. Betty's food has had a high reputation for many years, and now she has a coveted Michelin star and the assistance of son Graeme. Betty and Graeme remain behind the scenes while Eric in his Clan Ranald tartan kilt is your most congenial host. The two big lounges have lots of comfortable chairs. All the bedrooms are cottagey in size but beautifully appointed, with lovely fabrics, quality furniture, and luxury bathrooms. My favorites are the snug attic rooms that look out over the loch. The suite of two small rooms enjoys loch views both from the bedroom and the sitting room and has an immaculate, large bathroom. The two ground floor bedrooms are ideal for those who have difficulty with stairs. Two additional, very simple rooms are in a cottage to the rear of the hotel. The road runs in front of the hotel but this is not a problem since there is not much traffic in this quiet part of the world. A small passenger ferry sails from Port Appin to the Isle of Lismore while cars sail from Oban. From Oban you can also make a daytrip to the Isle of Mull. *Directions:* Port Appin is 2 miles off the A828, 25 miles north of Oban.

THE AIRDS HOTEL
Owners: Betty, Eric & Graeme Allen
Port Appin
Argyll PA38 4DF
tel (063173) 236 fax (063173) 535
14 rooms
From £90 per person, dinner, B & B
Closed January & February
Credit cards: none
Children welcome

Surrounded by 40 acres of grounds, the Rothes Glen Hotel was designed by the architect who built Balmoral, the Scottish royal residence. Its turrets and towers give the hotel the feeling of a baronial castle. Many of the original furnishings, a number of tapestries, high, ornate ceilings, and lovely, rich wooden doors remain to enhance the residents' lounge, bar, and dining room. The 16 bedrooms are attractively furnished and modernized with mini-bars, electric blankets, and radios. Room 44 is the grandest bedroom, with large windows and ornate French antique furniture. The Carmichael family have owned the castle for five generations and take great pride in providing a "home away from home" for their guests. They personally supervise the meals which frequently feature freshly caught fish as well as excellent Angus beef. Whisky has been distilled in this area for many years and it seems as though there is a distillery around every corner in this region. Several of the plants are open for tours and sampling of the product. *Directions:* Rothes Glen is 50 miles west of Inverness on the A94, 2 miles before the village of Rothes.

ROTHES GLEN HOTEL
Owners: Donald & Elaine Carmichael
Rothes
Morayshire IV33 7AH
tel (03403) 254
16 rooms
Single from £72, Double from £108
Closed January
Credit cards: all major
Children welcome

True seclusion and tranquility await you at Kinloch Lodge: there is a feeling of being miles from civilization.   The lodge dates from 1680 and it was here that Sir Alexander Macdonald decided that the Macdonalds would not send an army to help Bonnie Prince Charlie at Culloden--a decision which contributed to the Scots' defeat and the destruction of the clan system.   Today Claire and Godfrey Macdonald (Lord and Lady Macdonald) run the lodge as a small country house hotel.   A casual, easy atmosphere pervades the two small drawing rooms with their comfortable groupings of chairs and sofas.   The bedrooms have a light decor which helps the smaller rooms appear more spacious--all have either an en-suite bathroom or exclusive use of a bathroom across the hall.   The dining room is the most formal room, its polished tables neatly laid with silver and glass.   Claire Macdonald and Peter Macpherson provide quite the nicest food you will get on Skye.   Children unable to sit through a long, formal dinner will be served high tea. Godfrey Macdonald will direct you to his ancestral residence, Armadale Castle, where you can visit the Clan Donald Centre.   No visit to the island is complete without sampling Talisker whisky, the product of Skye's distillery at the head of Loch Bracadale.   *Directions:* Take the ferry from Kyle of Lochalsh to Skye, then the A850 to the A851 towards Armadale: turn left to Kinloch Lodge after 6 miles.

KINLOCH LODGE
Owners: Claire & Godfrey Macdonald
Sleat
Isle Of Skye IV43 8QY
tel (04713) 214/333
10 rooms
Single from £65, Double from £130
Open mid-March to November
Credit cards: MC VS
Children welcome

The rugged Isle of Mull with its tiny ports and breathtaking views is a fascinating place to explore.   Robin and Sue Blockley fell in love with the island, bought this spacious house with its large gardens and spectacular view, and decided to open it as a hotel.   Tironan House is a luxurious, tranquil haven amidst Mull's stark beauty.   Six bedrooms are in the main house and three in adjacent little cottages. The house is filled with lovely furniture and fires burn cheerfully in the grates of the cozy front and back sitting rooms.   Dinner is served in the large conservatory, its roof festooned by a grape-filled vine, where Sue provides a different menu every night and Robin works diligently making certain that guests are well taken care of. Mull has tremendously varied scenery, from craggy hills with tumbling waterfalls to island-dotted lochs, and the countryside is open for walking.   Nearby places of interest include Torosay Castle with its glorious gardens, Duart Castle, and Tobermoray, a charming yachting center.   Boats go to Staffa where you can visit the mighty Fingal's Cave which inspired Mendelssohn and Iona, the holy island of St Columba and burial place of Scottish, Norwegian, and Irish kings.   *Directions:* It is a 45-minute ferry crossing from Oban to Mull.   Turn left off the ferry on the Iona road.   After 15 miles turn right on the B8035 to Gruline.   After 5 miles, at the large yellow gate, turn left for the 1-mile drive to Tironan House.

TIRONAN HOUSE
Owners: Sue & Robin Blockley
Tironan, Isle of Mull
Argyll PA39 6ES
tel & fax (06815) 232
9 rooms
From £85 per person, dinner, B & B
Open June through September
Credit cards: none
Children over 10

Medwyn House is the perfect place to stay for exploring Edinburgh (a 45-minute drive to the north) and the River Tweed Valley with its woolen mills, ancient ruined abbeys, and grand variety of historic houses and castles. Anne and Mike Waterston fell in love with the house long before they realized what it would cost to heat its vast rooms. Undeterred by the expense, they ensure that central heating keeps guests warm so that they can enjoy the spaciousness of this lovely house. The pine-panelled hall and lounge rise to the eaves of what was once a 14th-century inn--a blazing log fire with deep, country-style chairs drawn around it give this room a mellow warmth. The adjacent large, sunny drawing room was added in the 1860s and has large sash windows with views of the garden. Three of the bedrooms are very large and have enormous bathrooms, while the other three are snug rooms located in an adjoining cottage. Anne, who has a particularly bubbly personality, enjoys looking after people and cooking them a lovely meal such as pasta with asparagus, carrot and ginger soup, leg of lamb with fresh vegetables, and, for dessert, lemon galette. Mike always adds a particularly welcome touch of cleaning guests' windscreens. *Directions:* From Edinburgh take the A702 towards Abington, go through West Linton, and take a right-hand turn signposted Baddingsgill/Golf Club. The house is on your right.

MEDWYN HOUSE
Owners: Anne & Mike Waterston
Medwyn Road
West Linton
Peeblesshire EH46 7HB
tel (0968) 60542 fax (0968) 60005
6 rooms & self-catering cottage
From £30 per person B & B
Closed mid-January to end-February
Children over 12 or by arrangement

If you have a Michelin map of Scotland, you will be able to find not only Whitebridge but also Knockie Lodge three quarters of the way down the southern shores of Loch Ness.   This lovely home is one of those places that has an end-of-the-earth feel to it--it is hard to believe that the problems and hustle and bustle of the world exist as you sit in the sunlounge and gaze across Loch Nan Lann at heather-covered hills.   It's a lovely view at any time but magnificent when the sun sets, flaming gold and red.   A houseparty atmosphere prevails as guests join one another (or sit in separate groups) at polished antique tables whose candlelit patina reflects crystal goblets and silver service.   The bedrooms are especially nicely decorated, varying in size from small (less expensive--contact hotel directly for these rates) through medium sized to Lovat, Grant, and Spruce, large, lovely rooms with exquisite views of the loch and mountains.   Guests use Knockie Lodge as a base for touring the Highlands, venturing as far afield as Skye and Ullapool, or staying closer to home with Culloden Battlefield, and Highland castles and glens. *Directions:* From Edinburgh taking the M90 to Perth and the A9 to Daviot (just south of Inverness) where you turn left towards Fort Augustus.   Pass through Whitebridge, and after 2 miles take a right-hand turn to Knockie Lodge.

KNOCKIE LODGE
Owners: Brenda & Ian Milward
Whitebridge
Inverness-shire IV1 2UP
tel (04563) 276   fax (04563) 389
10 rooms
Single from £75, Double from £150
*   Dinner, B & B*
Open May to October
Credit cards: all major
Children over 10

212

Hotels in Wales

The Old Bull's Head has a long and interesting history. The walls of its traditional beamed bar are decorated with antique weaponry and the town's ancient ducking chair provides a most unusual curio. Guests have the use of a large sitting room with flowery, chintz-covered chairs. Tasty pub food is served in the bar while the upstairs dining room serves more elaborate fare prepared by chef/proprietor Keith Rothwell. His partner, David Robertson, takes care of front of house. Charles Dickens stayed here, hence most bedrooms are named after Dickens characters. Each room is decorated differently, with matching drapes and bedspread and often coordinating wallpaper and armchair. All have modern bathrooms, television, and phone and either a lovely antique brass or iron bed. Castle Street which has lots of attractive shops and an old jail leads to Beaumaris Castle, a squat concentric fortification commissioned by Edward II. Nearby the Marquis of Anglesey's house and gardens are open to the public. Past Bangor, on the mainland, is Caernarfon Castle where Prince Charles was invested as Prince of Wales. *Directions:* From Chester take the A55, coast road, to Anglesey and cross on the Britannia Road Bridge. Then follow the A545 to Beaumaris.

THE OLD BULL'S HEAD
Owners: David Robertson & Keith Rothwell
Castle Street
Beaumaris
Isle of Anglesey
Gwynedd L158 8HU
tel (0248) 810329 fax (0248) 811294
11 rooms
Single from £40, Double from £65
Open all year
Credit cards: MC VS
Children welcome

Tucked away in a fold of green hills, The West Arms nestles in one of the loveliest valleys in Wales. The low-ceilinged, heavily beamed reception/sitting room welcomes you with logs blazing in the inglenook fireplace and a settle and pink-and-green-chintz-covered chairs drawn round the fire. In the adjacent parlor the same warm fabric has been used for the chairs while the walls have been painted a dark apple green. The dining room, too, has a large inglenook fireplace and ancient beams. Narrow, uneven stairs lead up to the most charming bedrooms with sloping ceilings and beamed walls. I preferred rooms facing the front of the inn to the large suite which does not have as high a standard of decor. (In addition there are several very plain, modern rooms.) While Chester and all the attractions of north Wales are easily accessible, there is delightful scenery close at hand. Little lanes take you up and around Lake Vyrnwy and down stunning valleys to Dinas Mawddy or Llanuwchllyn. When travelling to the attractive town of Llangollen, head cross country from Glyn Ceirrog following signs for the mine museum and then straight up and over the mountain--the views are stunning. *Directions:* Turn off the A5 at Chirk (midway between Oswestry and Llangollen) and follow the B4500 along the Ceiriog valley for 10 miles to Llanarmon Dyffryn Ceiriog.

THE WEST ARMS
Owner: Tim Alexandra
Llanarmon Dyffryn Ceiriog
near Llangollen
Clwyd LL20 7LD
tel (069) 176665   fax (069) 176622
14 rooms
Single from £49.50, Double from £78
Open all year
Credit cards: all major
Children welcome

Peter and Bridget Kindred bought Tyddyn Llan as a rundown farmhouse and have turned it into a delightful hotel with three cozy, informal sitting rooms, a tiny bar, and two interconnecting dining rooms decked out in blue and gold. A chef has replaced Bridget in the kitchen so both she and Peter are on hand to see that everything runs smoothly. Because the hotel was full we were unable to see rooms other than our own, a very comfortable, spacious twin-bedded room decorated in country-house style with a large clawfoot tub in the bathroom. Fishing is available on 4 miles of the nearby River Dee. Llandrillo was an important point on the drovers' route which was used for hundreds of years for driving livestock from Welsh farms to the markets in England. You can hike the old drovers' roads and tramp into the nearby Berwyn mountains. On nearby Lake Bala, the largest natural lake in Wales, you can sail, canoe, windsurf, or row. Steam trains run on a narrow track down one side of the lake. A more scenic train ride is from Blaenau Ffestiniog, a slate town where slate crags overhang the houses, to Porthmadog on the coast. On the way to the train visit Llechwedd slate caverns. Many visitors head into the walled city of Chester with its half-timbered shops. *Directions:* Tyddyn Llan is near Llandrillo, on the B4401 between Corwen (A5) and Bala.

TYDDYN LLAN
Owners: Bridget & Peter Kindred
Llandrillo
near Corwen
Clwyd LL21 0ST
tel & fax (04908) 264
10 rooms
Single from £47, Double from £74
Open all year
Credit cards: MC VS
Children welcome

Sitting high above the River Conwy, overlooking the ramparts of Conwy Castle across the broad river estuary, The Old Rectory offers guests hospitality, dinner with fellow guests, and the chance to learn a little about the Welsh and their culture; a harpist often plays and the Vaughans' son entertains guests with a few songs in Welsh before they go in to dinner. The long dining table is elegantly set with crystal and silver, the polished wood floors are covered with lovely patterned carpets, and fine watercolors hang on the walls. After dinner Michael and Wendy join their guests in the pine-panelled drawing room. Bedrooms, though not large, are well equipped with an iron and small ironing board, TV, telephone, and mineral water. Walnut and Mahogany rooms have splendid views to the castle and Mahogany has a half-tester bed and a bathroom with a large, bright, peacock-blue tub in the corner. Glorious Bodnant Gardens, best know for its azaleas and rhododendrons, is just down the road while also nearby is the attractive, well preserved medieval town of Conwy with its dramatic castle. Beyond lie all the rugged delights of Snowdonia. *Directions:* The Old Rectory is half a mile south of Conwy on the A470, just a one-and-a-half-hour drive from Manchester airport.

THE OLD RECTORY
Owners: Michael & Wendy Vaughan
Llanrwst Road
Llansanffraid Glan Conwy
Gwynedd LL28 5LF
tel (0492) 580611 fax (0492) 584555
4 rooms
From £20 to £40 per person B & B
Open February to 7th December
Credit cards: MC VS
Children over 10

I always hope that a beautiful region and a beautiful hotel will coincide and such is the case here. Snowdonia provides the most beautiful of Welsh scenery and Bodysgallen Hall provides the most beautiful of Welsh hotels. Built around a 13th-century watchtower and overlooking Conwy Castle, this large, rambling hotel looks surprisingly uniform, considering six centuries of additions, alterations and restorations. The mellow elegance and character of the house are preserved throughout. The spacious, dark-oak-panelled Jacobean entrance hall and the drawing room on the first floor have large fireplaces, mullioned windows, and comfortable furniture that create a warm, relaxed atmosphere. Nineteen beautiful bedrooms are found in the main house: none of the rooms are large, neither are their bathrooms, but they are all decorated to the highest of standards--I particularly enjoyed my stay in room 8 which has a sitting nook and the loveliest of views of the gardens. Nine suites are located in adjoining little cottages. The grounds are an absolute delight, a series of gardens divided by stone walls into "rooms." If you wish to leave the grounds, you have plenty to do: the hotel has outlined three daytrips into northern Wales. *Directions:* Take the A55 from Chester to the roundabout on the outskirts of Conwy where you turn right on the A470. The hotel entrance is on your right just over a mile from the roundabout.

BODYSGALLEN HALL
Manager: Richard Carr
Llandudno
Gwynedd LL30 1RS
tel (0492) 584466 fax (0492) 617163
28 rooms
Single from £88, Double from £120
Open all year
Credit cards: all major
Children over 8

This hotel has a superb location high in the mid-Wales mountains at the head of Lake Vyrnwy overlooking miles and miles of pine-forested mountaintops. A decidedly old-fashioned feeling permeates the building, from the pine-panelled entrance hall to the drawing room with its ornate ceiling, grand piano, and large windows opening up to views of the lake stretching into the distance with pine-forested hills rising from its shore. The bar and dining room share the same stunning view: sunsets are dramatic. Bedrooms face either the lake or the driveway behind the hotel--it is well worth the extra pounds to secure a bedroom with a lake view. The tavern that lies beyond the hotel has a juke box and games room that introduce a rather jarring note into otherwise idyllically peaceful surroundings. Walking and relaxing are the most popular pastimes. The lake is stocked with 5,000 trout every year and over 10,000 pheasants are released during the shooting season. Tennis and sailing are available for guests. *Directions:* Lake Vyrnwy is a one-hour drive from Shrewsbury--take the A458 towards Welshpool and just after Ford take the B4393 to Lake Vyrnwy. The hotel's driveway is on the right 400 yards after the dam.

LAKE VYRNWY HOTEL
Manager: Jim Talbot
Lake Vyrnwy
Llanwddyn
Clwyd SY10 0LY
tel (069) 173692 fax (069) 173259
30 rooms
Single from £46, Double from £68.50
Open all year
Credit cards: all major
Children welcome

This ivy-covered inn sitting at the center of this tiny Welsh village is an old and long-established sporting inn. The small, cozy bars have lots of charm, with exposed stonework, old beams, and open fireplaces where cheery fires burn on chilly winter evenings. In the sporting tradition of this pub, bedrooms are named after and marked by a different fishing fly. All but two are above and behind the inn, in a quite modern addition which blocks noise from the bar. Rooms are very pleasantly though simply decorated. Guests can dine in the cozy little country-style dining room or at a table in the bar and fresh fish or game, according to the season, are always on the menu. Fishing and shooting are arranged by Richard and the inn's full time ghillie and keeper. They are well versed in their mile-and-a-half stretch of the Wye and take pride in assisting their sporting visitors to make full use of their fishing and shooting facilities. (With advanced notice Richard can also arrange demonstrations of gun-dog training.) The upper Wye valley is unspoilt and serene and Di directs guests on countryside walks through its pretty scenery. Hay-on-Wye, the attractive market town famous for its many second-hand bookshops, is just 7 miles away. *Directions:* The Griffin Inn is located in the center of Llyswen, on the A470 Buith Wells road, 9 miles from Brecon.

THE GRIFFIN INN
Owners: Di & Richard Stockton
Llyswen
Brecon
Powys LD3 0YP
tel (0874) 754241
8 rooms
Single from £32, Double from £55
Open all year
Credit cards: all major
Children welcome

This grand and dignified house was designed by Sir Clough Ellis (of fanciful Portmeirion) and rescued from ruin by Sir Bernard Ashley (of Laura Ashley). The lounging rooms are a delight: a great hall with an open fire, antiques, huge sofas, and interesting pictures, a flowery sitting room, and a book-filled library with leather chairs and a snooker table.   Each bedroom or suite is individually planned and quite different from the next--some are very flowery, others very masculine. The suites are up two long flights of stairs under the eaves.   The smaller rooms of the north wing are most attractive--several have small four-poster beds and Welsh mineral water, sherry, heart-shaped shortbread biscuits, and fluffy robes are provided.   Mark Salter and his young kitchen staff won the Welsh Restaurant of the year award within six months of opening.   The Wye River valley offers several places of interest and nearby are the ruins of Tintern Abbey, celebrated by Wordsworth.   You can visit Hereford, a lovely, sleepy, medieval city astride the River Wye, its cathedral built in several styles from the 11th century, and Hay-on-Wye with its many bookstores.   There is an abundance of pretty countryside, from the stark beauty of the Brecon Beacons to the soft prettiness of the Wye valleys. *Directions:* Llangoed Hall is on the A470, midway between Buith Wells and Brecon.

LLANGOED HALL
Manager: Tom Ward
Llyswen
Brecon
Powys LD3 0YP
tel (0874) 754525 fax (0874) 754545
23 rooms
Single from £95, Double from £115
Open all year
Credit cards: all major
Children over 8

A soft pink colorwash brightens the exterior of this spacious home in the village of Newport. Cnapan House is very much a family-run affair, with John and Eluned Lloyd, their daughter Judith, and her husband Michael Cooper extending a warm welcome. John and Michael are your genial hosts while Eluned and Judith work together in the kitchen. Lunchtime fare emphasizes wholefood cooking with old-fashioned, hearty soups and puddings. Tables are covered with lace cloths for dinner, adding a romantic touch to a special meal where the main course is always served with five or six vegetables. Guests can enjoy before-dinner drinks in either the sitting room or the bar: both snug rooms filled with country antiques and overflowing with charm. The bedrooms are superb, artfully decorated in a light, airy style and immaculately furnished, with every nook and cranny filled with old family treasures. One guestroom is a family room with a small adjoining bunk-bedroom for the children. (Nursery teas are served in the early evening so that parents can put the children in bed or in front of the TV before coming down to dinner.) You will love the welcoming, free-and-easy atmosphere that pervades this home. *Directions:* Newport is on the A487 11 miles west of Cardigan and 7 miles east of Fishguard.

CNAPAN HOUSE
Owners: The Lloyd & Cooper families
East Street
Newport
Pembrokeshire SA42 0WF
tel (0239) 820575
5 rooms
From £21 per person B & B
Closed February
Credit cards: MC VS
Children welcome

Soughton Hall is a spectacular, stately mansion approached down an impressive avenue of towering lime trees and surrounded by 150 acres of parkland. This former Bishops' Palace was in an almost hopeless state of disrepair when it was purchased by John and Rosemary Rodenhurst who have done a sensational job of returning it to its former glory. On the ground floor are a bar, panelled library with leather chairs, and a cozy reception lounge where a log fire blazes cheerfully in winter. Upstairs the lofty dining room and imposing drawing room with its tapestry-hung walls and formal furniture give the impression that this is a place of hushed formality, but this is not the case for John, Rosemary, and their son Simon ensure that there is not a trace of stuffiness. I preferred the "ordinary" bedrooms to the suites and the Garden Room with its spiral staircase and greenhouse bathroom. Breakfast is served in a delightful, country-pine room near the kitchen which was formerly the servants' hall. Simon provides instruction for day tours, from Chester to Snowdonia, that give you the excuse to stay for a week. *Directions:* Leave the A55 (Chester to Conwy road) at the A5119 signposted Mold and after 1 mile follow signs to the left for Soughton Hall.

SOUGHTON HALL
Owners: The Rodenhurst family
Northop
near Mold
Clwyd CH7 6AB
tel (0352) 86811 fax (0352) 86382
12 rooms
Single from £100, Double from £140
* (Dinner, B & B)*
Open all year
Credit cards: all major
Children over 12

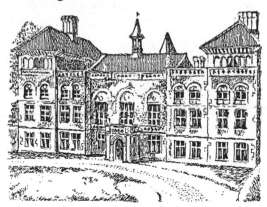

Portmeirion is the dream of architect Sir Clough Ellis who bought this wooded hillside overlooking Tremadog Bay and built an Italianate fantasy village because he adored the Mediterranean fishing village of Portofino. It has ornate, color-washed houses and cottages, a campanile, sculptures, gardens of sub-tropical plants, and architectural oddments from all over Britain. Down by the sea, away from the visitors who come to Portmeirion every day, behind the facade of a seemingly unpretentious Victorian exterior, is the luxurious Portmeirion Hotel. The public rooms of the hotel are a decorator's extravaganza: a bright turquoise sitting room, a glittering Indian bar, a maharajah-style dining room, and a wicker and marble, Chinese-motif dining room. There are fourteen bedrooms in the main house and twenty more in cottages throughout the village. The most elaborate, and the most frequently requested, are the Indian Room with its four-poster bed constructed from the bases of Indian table lamps and the Peacock Suite. There is a delightful fantasy feel to the whole place as you stroll the winding, cobbled streets in the quiet of an evening and gaze out across the vast, sandy estuary to distant hills. Remind yourself that you are in Wales by making excursions to some of its castles or ride aboard one of its narrow-gauge railways from nearby Porthmadog. *Directions:* Portmeirion is south of Minffordd which is on the A487, 5 miles from Porthmadog.

PORTMEIRION HOTEL
Manager: Mennai Williams
Portmeirion
Gwynedd LL48 6ET
tel (0766) 770228 fax (0766) 771331
20 rooms village, 14 rooms hotel
Village Double from £67
Hotel Double from £101
Closed last 3 weeks January
Credit cards: all major
Children welcome in village rooms

Key Map

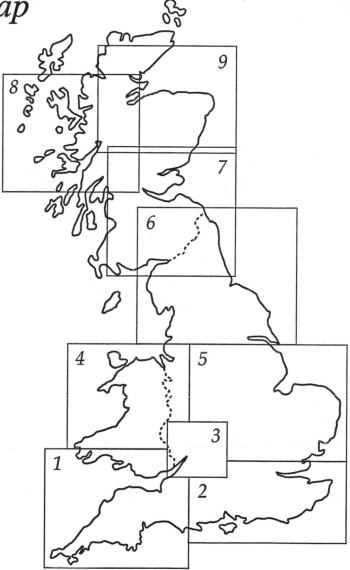

Map 1

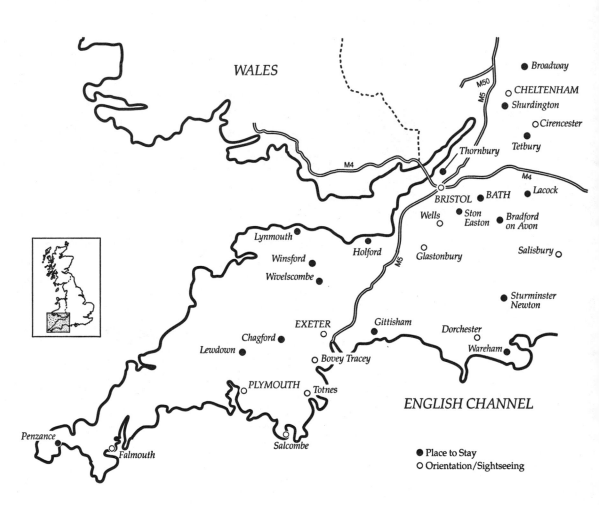

WALES

Broadway
CHELTENHAM
Shurdington
Cirencester
Tetbury
Thornbury

M50
M5
M4

BRISTOL • BATH
Lacock
M4
Wells • Ston
Easton
Bradford
on Avon

Lynmouth
Holford
Glastonbury
Salisbury

Winsford
Wivelscombe

Sturminster
Newton

EXETER
Gittisham
Dorchester
Chagford
Wareham
Lewdown
Bovey Tracey

PLYMOUTH
Totnes

ENGLISH CHANNEL

Penzance

Falmouth
Salcombe

● Place to Stay
O Orientation/Sightseeing

Map 2

Broadway

Buckland

Woodstock

Burford

OXFORD

Aylesbury

Aston Clinton

Great Milton

Henley on-Thames

M40

M1

A1

M11

○ CAMBRIDGE

Lavenham

Hintlesham

Dedham

Colchester ○

IPSWICH

M25

M4

LONDON

Hurstbourne Tarrant

M3

M25

M25

M2

M20

Canterbury

Winchester

M23

Ashford

Salisbury ○

East Grinstead

Rushlake Green

Cranbrook

Rye

Sturminster Newton

SOUTHAMPTON

M27

Storrington

Battle

New Milton

Climping

BRIGHTON

Wareham

PORTSMOUTH

ENGLISH CHANNEL

● Place to Stay
○ Orientation/Sightseeing

Map 3

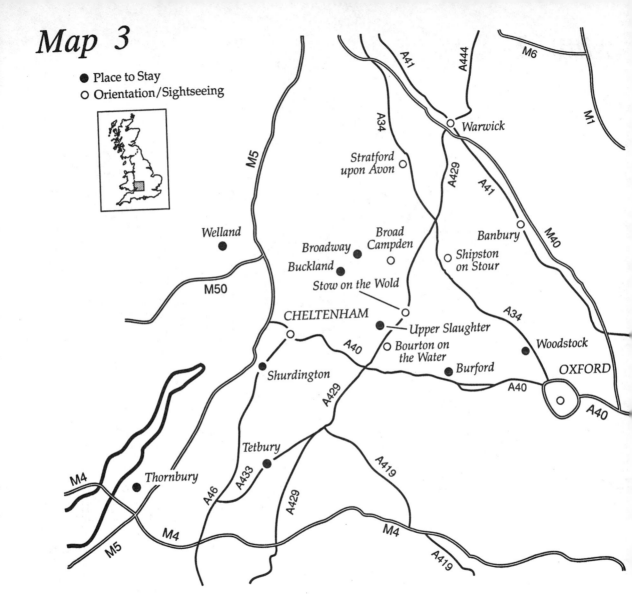

- ● Place to Stay
- ○ Orientation/Sightseeing

Welland ●

Broadway ●
Buckland ●
Broad Campden ○

Stratford upon Avon ○

Banbury ○
Shipston on Stour ○

Stow on the Wold ○

CHELTENHAM ○
Upper Slaughter ●
Bourton on the Water ○
Burford ●
Woodstock ●
OXFORD ○

Shurdington ●

Tetbury ●
Thornbury ●

M5
M50
M4
M6
M1
M40
M4
A41
A444
A34
A429
A41
A34
A40
A429
A419
A46
A433
A429

Map 4

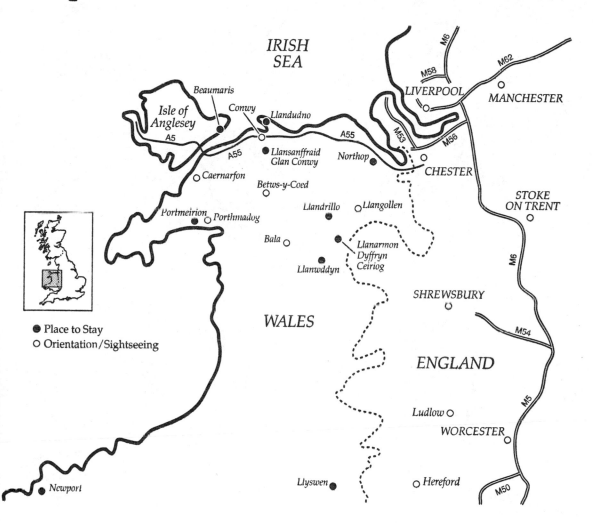

IRISH
SEA

Isle of
Anglesey

Beaumaris

Conwy

Llandudno

A5

A55

Llansanffraid
Glan Conwy

Betws-y-Coed

Caernarfon

Northop

A55

M6

M58

M62

LIVERPOOL

MANCHESTER

M53

M56

CHESTER

STOKE
ON TRENT

Portmeirion   Porthmadog

Llandrillo

Llangollen

Bala

Llanarmon
Dyffryn
Ceiriog

Llanwddyn

M6

SHREWSBURY

● Place to Stay
○ Orientation/Sightseeing

WALES

ENGLAND

M54

Ludlow

WORCESTER

M5

Newport

Llyswen

Hereford

M50

229

Map 5

Map 6

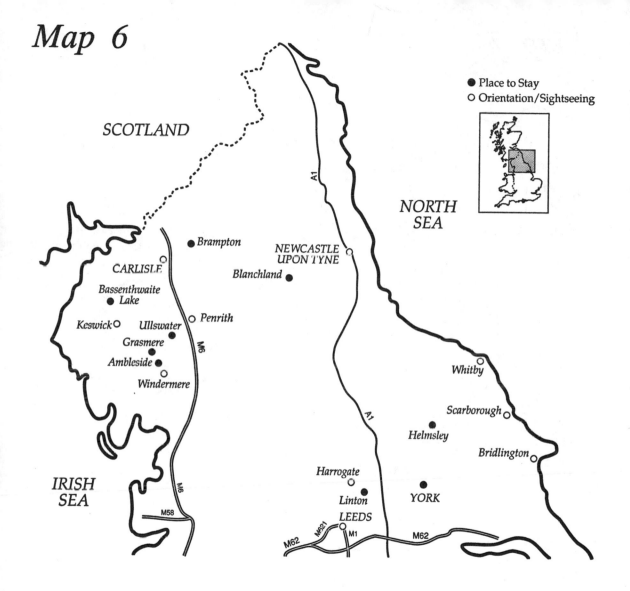

SCOTLAND

NORTH SEA

● Place to Stay
○ Orientation/Sightseeing

● Brampton

NEWCASTLE UPON TYNE ○

○ CARLISLE

Blanchland ●

Bassenthwaite Lake ●

Keswick ○

Ullswater ●

○ Penrith

Grasmere ●

M6

Ambleside ●

○ Windermere

Whitby ○

Scarborough ○

Helmsley ●

Bridlington ○

IRISH SEA

Harrogate ○

Linton ●

YORK ●

LEEDS ○

A1

A1

M6

M58

M62 M621 M1 M62

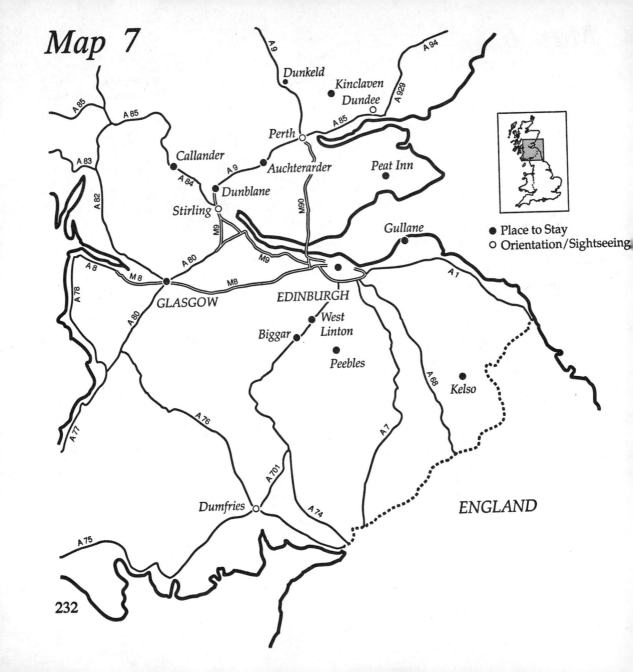

Map 7

A 94

A 9

Dunkeld

Kinclaven

Dundee

A 929

A 85

A 85

A 85

A 83

Callander

Perth

A 9

Auchterarder

Peat Inn

A 84

Dunblane

A 82

Stirling

M90

Gullane

M9

● Place to Stay
○ Orientation/Sightseeing

A 80

M9

A 8

A 78

M 8

A 80

M 8

EDINBURGH

A 1

GLASGOW

West
Linton

Biggar

A 68

A 80

Peebles

Kelso

A 77

A 76

A 7

A 701

ENGLAND

Dumfries

A 74

A 75

Map 8

Ullapool

Isle of Skye

Nairn

A 835

A 96

Inverness

Drumnadrochit

Sleat

A 87

A 82

Whitebridge

Ardvasar

A 9

Mallaig

A 830

A 82

Fort William

• Place to Stay
○ Orientation/Sightseeing

Loch Sunart

Isle of Mull

A 82

Port Appin

Pitlochry

Aberfeldy

A 828

Tironan

A 85

Oban

A 85

A 84

Auchterarder

Callander

A 9

A 83

Dunblane

A 816

A 82

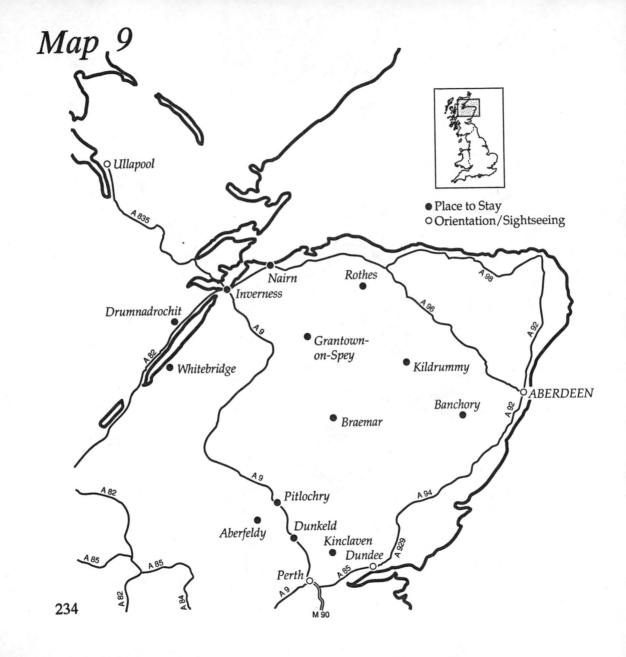

Map 9

Ullapool

A 835

Nairn

Rothes

A 98

Inverness

A 96

Drumnadrochit

A 92

Grantown-
on-Spey

Kildrummy

A 82

Whitebridge

A 9

ABERDEEN

Banchory

A 92

Braemar

A 94

A 9

Pitlochry

A 82

A 929

Aberfeldy

Dunkeld

A 85

Kinclaven

A 85

Dundee

Perth

A 85

A 82

A 9

A 84

234

M 90

● Place to Stay
○ Orientation/Sightseeing

U. S. Hotel Representatives

(Alphabetical Order)

American Wolfe International
800-223-5695

London, Capital Hotel, 107
London, L'Hotel, 112

Best Western Hotels
800-528-1234

Kildrummy, Kildrummy Castle Hotel, 198
Kinclaven, Ballathie House, 199
Winsford, Royal Oak Inn, 171

Forte Hotels
800-223-5672

Helmsley, The Black Swan, 146
Lavenham, The Swan Hotel, 151
Woodstock, The Bear Hotel, 173

Josephine Barr
800-323-5463

Josephine Barr often answers the phone. She is very familiar with all her hotels.

Ambleside, Rothay Manor, 118
Auchterarder, Auchterarder House, 180
Bath, The Queensberry Hotel, 126
Callander, Roman Camp Hotel, 185

Edinburgh, The Howard, 189
Kelso, Sunlaws House Hotel, 197
London, Dorset Square Hotel, 108
Whitebridge, Knockie Lodge, 211
Wivelscombe, Langley House, 172
Woodstock, The Feathers, 174
York, The Grange, 175

Leading Hotels of the World
800-223-6800

Broadway, The Lygon Arms, 132
London, Connaught Hotel, 108
New Milton, Chewton Glen, 156

Pride of Britain Hotels
Abercrombie & Kent
800-323-7308

Pride of Britain is a consortium of owner-managed country house hotels in Britain. Their U. S. marketing and publicity is handled by Abercrombie & Kent. They will give you toll free telephone numbers that enable you to dial each hotel directly to make your reservations.

Aberfeldy, Farlayer House, 178
Battle, Netherfield Place, 128
Bradford-on-Avon, Woolley Grange, 130
Dedham, Maison Talbooth, 138
Dunblane, Cromlix House, 187
Gittisham, Combe House Hotel, 140
Glasgow, One Devonshire Gardens, 193
Grasmere, Michael's Nook, 141

Grimston, Congham Hall, 144
Gullane, Greywalls, 195
Hurstbourne Tarrant, Essebourne Manor, 149
Lewdown, Lewtrenchard Manor, 152
London, The Beaufort, 105
London, Dorset Square Hotel, 108
Matlock, Riber Hall, 155
Shurdington, The Greenway, 160
Storrington, Little Thakeham, 162
Sturminster Newton, Plumber Manor, 163
Thornbury, Thornbury Castle, 165
Whitebridge, Knockie Lodge, 211

Rank Hotels
800-223-5560

London, Athenaeum Hotel & Apartments, 104

Relais & Chateaux
800-677-3524

Relais & Chateaux is a worldwide association of fine hotels and restaurants. Their U.S. booking agent, charges a $15 "file fee" for each vacation.

Aston Clinton, The Bell Inn, 120
Brampton, Farlan Hall, 131
Chagford, Gidleigh Park, 135
East Grinstead, Gravetye Manor, 139
Fort William, Inverlochy Castle, 192
Great Milton, Le Manoir aux Quat' Saisons, 143
Hambleton, Hambleton Hall, 145
London, Capital Hotel, 107

New Milton, Chewton Glen, 156
Port Appin, The Airds Hotel, 206
Ston Easton, Ston Easton Park, 161
Ullswater, Sharrow Bay Hotel, 166

Small Luxury Hotels
800-544-7570

Auchterarder, Auchterarder House, 180
Aylesbury, Hartwell House, 121
Banchory, Invery House, 181
Bath, The Royal Crescent Hotel, 127
Hintlesham, Hintlesham Hall, 147
Llandudno, Bodysgallen Hall, 218
Llyswen, Llangoed Hall, 221
London, Dukes Hotel, 110
London, The Stafford, 114
Tetbury, The Close, 164
Upper Slaughter, Lords of the Manor Hotel, 167
York, Middlethorpe Hall, 176

Utell International
800-448-8355

Bath, The Royal Crescent Hotel, 127
Lavenham, The Swan Hotel, 151
London, Athenaeum Hotel & Apartments, 104
London, The Beaufort, 105
London, Brown's Hotel, 106
London, Dukes Hotel, 110
London, The Stafford, 114

Index

DISCOVERIES FROM OUR READERS

"Discoveries from Our Readers" features places to stay that sound excellent, but which we have not yet had an opportunity to visit. If you have a favorite hideaway that you would be willing to share with other readers, we would love to hear from you. The type of accommodations we feature are those with old world ambiance, special charm, and warmth of welcome. Please send the following information:

1. *Your name, address and telephone number.*

2. *Name, address and telephone number of your discovery.*

3. *Rate for a double room including tax, service and breakfast.*

4. *Brochure or picture (we cannot return material).*

5. *Permission to use an edited version of your description.*

6. *Would you want your name, city, and state included in the book?*

Please send to:

Karen Brown's Country Inn Guides, Post Office Box 70, San Mateo, CA 94401, USA
Telephone (415) 342-5591   Fax (415) 342-9153

Karen Brown's Country Inn Guides

The Most Reliable Series on Charming Places to Stay

KAREN BROWN'S
FRENCH
Country Inns & Itineraries

UPDATED AND REVISED · SIXTH EDITION

KAREN BROWN'S
CALIFORNIA
Country Inns & Itineraries

UPDATED AND REVISED · SECOND EDITION

KAREN BROWN'S
ITALIAN
Country Inns & Itineraries

UPDATED AND REVISED · FOURTH EDITION

KAREN BROWN'S
FRENCH
Country Bed & Breakfasts

UPDATED AND REVISED · SECOND EDITION

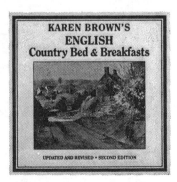

KAREN BROWN'S
ENGLISH
Country Bed & Breakfasts

UPDATED AND REVISED · SECOND EDITION

KAREN BROWN'S
GERMAN
Country Inns & Itineraries

UPDATED AND REVISED · THIRD EDITION

KAREN BROWN'S
ITALIAN
Country Bed & Breakfasts

NEW · FIRST EDITION

KAREN BROWN'S
ENGLISH, WELSH & SCOTTISH
Country Hotels & Itineraries

UPDATED AND REVISED · SIXTH EDITION

Order Form

KAREN BROWN'S COUNTRY INN GUIDES

Please ask in your local bookstore for **KAREN BROWN'S COUNTRY INN** guides.
If the books you want are unavailable, you may order directly from the publisher.

——— *Austrian Country Inns & Castles (1988 edition) $6.00*
——— *California Country Inns & Itineraries $14.95*
——— *English Country Bed & Breakfasts $13.95*
——— *English, Welsh & Scottish Country Hotels & Itineraries $14.95*
——— *French Country Bed & Breakfasts $13.95*
——— *French Country Inns & Itineraries $14.95*
——— *German Country Inns & Itineraries $14.95*
——— *Irish Country Inns (1988 edition) $6.00*
——— *Italian Country Bed & Breakfasts $13.95*
——— *Italian Country Inns & Itineraries $14.95*
——— *Portuguese Country Inns & Pousadas $12.95*
——— *Scandinavian Country Inns & Manors (1987 edition) $6.00*
——— *Spanish Country Inns & Paradors $12.95*
——— *Swiss Country Inns & Chalets (1989 edition) $6.00*

Name _____   Street _____

City _____ State _____ Zip _____ tel: _____

Credit Card (Mastercard or Visa) _____ Exp: _____

Add $3.50 for the first book and .50 for each additional book for postage & packing.
California residents add 8.25% sales tax.
Indicate number of copies of each title; send form with check or credit card information to:

KAREN BROWN'S COUNTRY INN GUIDES
Post Office Box 70, San Mateo, California, 94401, U.S.A.
Tel: (415) 342-9117   Fax: (415) 342-9153

Karen Brown's
English Country Bed & Breakfasts

The Choice of the Discriminating Traveller to England

Featuring the Most Charming Bed & Breakfasts

English Country Bed & Breakfasts is the perfect companion guide to *English, Welsh & Scottish Country Hotels & Itineraries.* Whereas the *English, Welsh & Scottish Country Hotels & Itineraries* book features wonderful small hotels and inns the Bed & Breakfast guide has our personal selection of places to stay in private homes, guesthouses, and pubs. All the pertinent information is given: a detailed description, nearby sightseeing, driving directions, sketch, price, owner's name, telephone and fax numbers, dates open, and acceptability of children.

English Country Bed & Breakfasts does not replace *English, Welsh & Scottish Country Hotels & Itineraries*--together they make the perfect pair for the traveller who wants to enjoy the comparatively low prices offered by travelling the bed & breakfast way. Both feature places to stay with charm, warmth of welcome, and old-world ambiance: *English Country Bed & Breakfasts* features places to stay in private homes, pubs and guesthouses; *English, Welsh & Scottish Country Hotels & Itineraries* features small hotels and inns PLUS the added bonus of driving itineraries, handy for use with the bed & breakfast guide. Each book uses the same maps so it is easy to choose a combination of places to stay from each, adding great variety for where to spend the night.

KAREN BROWN wrote her first travel guide, *French Country Inns & Chateaux*, in 1979. This original guide is now in its 6th edition plus 13 books have been added to the series which has become known as the most personalized, reliable reference library for the discriminating traveller. Although Karen's staff has expanded, she is still involved in the publication of her guide books. Karen, her husband, Rick, their daughter, Alexandra, and son, Richard, live on the coast south of San Francisco at their own country inn, Seal Cove Inn, in Moss Beach, California.

JUNE BROWN, CTC, born in Sheffield, England, has an extensive background in travel dating back to her school-girl days when she "youth hosteled" throughout Europe. When June moved to California, she worked as a travel consultant before joining her friend Karen to assist in the research, writing and production of her Country Inn guides. June now lives in the San Francisco Bay area with her husband, Tony, their teen-aged son, Simon, and young daughter, Clare.

BARBARA TAPP, the talented artist responsible for all of the hotel sketches and delightful illustrations in this guide, was raised in Australia where she studied in Sydney at the School of Interior Design. Although Barbara continues with freelance projects, she devotes much of her time to illustrating Karen's Country Inn guides. Barbara lives in the San Francisco Bay area with her husband, Richard, their two sons, Jonothan and Alexander, and young daughter, Georgia.

JANN POLLARD, the artist responsible for the beautiful painting on the cover of this guide, has studied art since childhood, and is well-known for her outstanding impressionistic-style water colors which she has exhibited in numerous juried shows, winning many awards. Jann travels frequently to Europe (using Karen Brown's guides) where she loves to paint old world architecture. Jann lives in the San Francisco Bay area with her husband, Gene, and two daughters.